TREND
WATCHING

TREND WATCHING

*How the Media
Create Trends
and How to be
the First to
Uncover Them*

John E. Merriam
and
Joel Makower

A Tilden Press Book

amacom

American Management Association

This book is available at a special
discount when ordered in bulk quantities.
For information, contact Special Sales Department,
AMACOM, a division of American Management Association,
135 West 50th Street, New York, NY 10020.

Library of Congress Cataloging-in-Publication Data

Merriam, John E.
    Trend watching.

    "A Tilden Press book."
    Includes index.
    1. Mass media—United States. 2. Mass media—
Methodology. I. Makower, Joel, 1952–
II. Title.
P92.U5M47   1987   302.2'34'0973   87-47828
ISBN 0-8144-5890-4

Printing number

10 9 8 7 6 5 4 3 2 1

Acknowledgments

Several people made valuable contributions to this book, for which they deserve recognition and thanks. Ann M. Welch of the Conference on Issues and Media helped to build the National Media Index, provided indispensable research, and produced the graphs that appear in this book. Linda F. Anderson, Laura A. Bergheim, and Patrick A. Tracey contributed valuable editorial and logistical support. Bill Hogan read an early draft of the manuscript and proffered extremely helpful suggestions. Gail Ross assisted with legal matters but, more important, was responsible for introducing the two authors. Nancy J. Brandwein's keen editorial instincts helped to organize the text and sharpen the focus. And Barbara Merriam, as always, gave her unfailing support, guidance, and counsel.

Thanks also are due to computer jockey Barry M. Webb, who designed the software behind the National Media Index; George Kroloff, a long-time supporter; and comments from the loyal readers of *Issues Management Letter*, who have proved that the ideas in this book work.

Preface

What's going on?

In the waning years of the twentieth century, this question has become more than just a breezy conversation starter. The challenge to comprehend all that is before us has become immense, at times overwhelming. It is no longer enough merely to stay current, which itself can be a time-consuming endeavor. To survive and thrive—personally, professionally, or politically—in the 1990s and beyond, it will be necessary to get ahead of the pack, to anticipate what's to come before such knowledge becomes conventional wisdom.

This is a book about understanding, analyzing, and anticipating "what's going on." It is about media and trends, and about how each affects—and is affected by—the other. It describes a system that can help you gain a sharper focus on how the world works, whether the "world" in question is a company, an industry, a region, or an idea.

This book was born of several forces, not the least of which was the fascination with trends brought about by the work of John Naisbitt, author of the best-selling book *Megatrends*. The success of Naisbitt's efforts clearly underscores the hunger for insight, for a life raft that might enable us to stay afloat amid the pounding waves of the sea of information that surrounds all of us.

But Naisbitt's work, however successful, must be seen as only a beginning. Naisbitt, after all, didn't invent the notion of trend analysis; he merely popularized it. Moreover, his wasn't the only school of trend-analysis thought. Many other individuals have been using newspapers and other media to track trends for years, often involving systems somewhat more sophisticated than those employed by the Naisbitt group. This is not to denigrate Naisbitt's techniques; they have clearly served a purpose.

Most important, the appetites whetted by *Megatrends* cannot be satisfied merely by understanding the "ten new directions transforming our lives," as Naisbitt described his book. While many individuals and organizations have found value in being told of the forces affecting them, many others want to find out for themselves. And not just the "megatrends"; there is an endless number of *micro*trends that can play key roles in the success of any endeavor, whether it is running a major business or running for public office. Indeed, it is the diversity of interests and pursuits in our increasingly complex world that makes it so exciting—and, at times, so frustrating—to be in business. No single set of analyses can possibly suffice for everyone.

This is where Trend Watching comes in. It is the product of a journalist and an issues analyst, in many ways the ideal combined perspective from which to view how the media affect trends and how trends affect the media.

Ultimately, the ideas in this book are based on work pioneered by John Merriam, whose interest in media and trends began in the 1970s at the World Bank, where he served under the bank's president, Robert S. McNamara, as head of its Department of Information and Public Affairs. As a public relations professional, Merriam, a former Foreign Service officer and political adviser, had been frustrated in his attempts to impress upon McNamara and other "numbers people" the impact of media coverage on a variety of issues. (Indeed, the numbers people were more inclined to view public relations types as "the guys who go to lunch for a living.") Merriam decided that public relations needed its own data base to quantify answers to the question, "What are the national media telling the American people?"

Those efforts led to Merriam's creation of the National Media Index, the first computerized data base to integrate broadcast and print sources into a single, numerically compatible index (more about which appears later in this book); and publication of two newsletters, *Issues Management Letter* and *Corporate Exposure*, by the Conference on Issues and Media, which Merriam founded in 1981. Through those newsletters—and the accompanying consulting and lecturing—Merriam developed and refined the ideas behind Trend Watching.

In the chapters that follow you will gain a fuller understanding of Merriam's system and how it can be used to, in effect, create your own customized set of "megatrends." Among other things, you will be shown how, through following a few relatively simple steps, you can make sense of the myriad streams of media information that flow across your desk. As you will see, you probably already are performing some of the key steps of Trend Watching when you consume newspapers, magazines, and news broadcasts on a regular basis. Through Trend Watching, you apply a few additional steps that will provide you with a unique data base from which you can make predictions about your areas of interest.

Before we begin with the business at hand, however, we wish to offer a warning: It is critical to understand that you will find little magic in your Trend-Watching numbers without some thoughtful analysis. Like any other data base, from sales spreadsheets to your local telephone directory, the value comes from the ways in which the data are used. As social scientist Theodore Roszak noted, there is a disturbing tendency to confuse "data" with "ideas" and "information" with "knowledge." Trend Watching will provide you with data and information, to be sure. The ideas and knowledge, however, must come from you.

Contents

1

The Value of Trend Watching

It all made so much sense. Although it hadn't yet been introduced, the new product already had worldwide name recognition, more so perhaps than any other product in history. Its parent company had proved itself a master of marketing. The company's commercials and theme songs typically had become part of the American vernacular; several years ago, one of its jingles was a Top-40 hit. The company's high-priced marketing gurus predicted that the new product would be embraced by the small but influential corps of young, upwardly mobile professionals, a key segment of the nation's movers and shakers. From there, the flames would be fanned by one of the most intensive ad and marketing campaigns ever, with coupons, giveaways, tastings, and publicity stunts galore. It would, everyone agreed, take off like wildfire.

But New Coke flickered, smoldered, and nearly died.

Those of us who analyze media coverage to track trends in American society could have saved the folks at Coca-Cola a lot of embarrassment—and more than a little money. If Coca-Cola officials had supplemented the company's intensive marketing studies with a much simpler technique of watching trends using news media, they might have realized that their gamble on the yuppie market was shaky at best.

Our trend data for the period clearly showed a strong conservative, almost nostalgic bent, a mood indicating that this was not a good time to try radical new ideas. Our tracking of the media found widespread satisfaction with the status quo. Among other things, Americans' criticism of government was at its lowest level in years. Even more significant, social concerns, morality, and family values were shown to be on the rise.

For more than six generations, Coca-Cola has had a special place in American homes. It is a bona fide American institution and, some would say, as symbolic of traditional American values as Sunday picnics and the Super Bowl. Coca-Cola executives failed to understand this, or to appreciate the impact they would create by, in effect, pulling this institution off the market and replacing it with a newfangled substitute. Coca-Cola's big mistake may not have been in making the change, but in making such a big deal of it. Ultimately, of course, Coca-Cola recovered—and actually increased its market share—by reintroducing the original as "Coke Classic" and letting both products vie for shelf space. Had this happy ending been calculated by Coca-Cola, the sequence of events would have been heralded as sheer genius. Instead, it was sheer luck.

And then there is Du Pont. In this day of health and environmental hazards—with Union Carbide, Dow, and virtually every other chemical company finding itself regularly battling regulators and reporters over some type of environmental contamination, industrial accident, or other calamity—Du Pont has scarcely a blemish to its name. Indeed, it has earned a reputation for disclosing things in a timely and positive manner, and has maintained an enviable relationship with reporters. In a world of industrial polluters and white-collar criminals, this multinational chemical company has managed to score such public relations triumphs as its highly visible campaign to save the bald eagle.

How does Du Pont do it? What Du Pont does is listen. For starters, the company set up a system whereby its 110,000 employees keep their ears to the tracks, listening carefully for what they believe are the problems the firm ought to be addressing. One widely hailed result of this program has been Du Pont's sensitivity to concerns of female employees. It began with an information campaign in the early 1980s to sensitize workers and supervisors to sexual harassment. The program expanded as women increasingly traveled for the company and encountered problems on the road. In 1986, there emerged a Rape Prevention and Personal Safety Program, again widely acclaimed by the media as well as by experts in the field.

While Coca-Cola's top brass used static marketing data to analyze product potential in age-old corporate fashion, Du Pont's leaders collected dynamic data from other sources to gauge their company's future. Indeed, Du Pont's ability to keep its antenna—actually, some 110,000 antennae—tuned into the changes in its world gives it the racer's edge in the fast-changing corporate environment of the late twentieth century.

Big companies like Du Pont (or, perhaps, Coca-Cola) can afford to set up elaborate systems for detecting and predicting changes in our society. After all, for what a thirty-second spot on "Wide World of Sports" costs, a firm can finance an impressive trend-spotting operation. Fortunately, the technology and techniques utilized by these firms can be used by just about any organization of any size, using such everyday "technology" as the daily newspaper, a pencil, a few sheets of paper, and the willingness to take a couple of small steps into the brave new world of the information age.

It's Called Trend Watching

What exactly is Trend Watching? It is deceptively simple. In its essence, Trend Watching involves reading (or watching) news media, counting issues and events, recording them for later examination, and using the data that result to formulate predictions about what may happen over the next one to five years.

If you are a regular reader of at least one newspaper and a magazine or two, you are already doing some of the first part, and you also perform the second in a fashion, unconsciously keeping track of which issues are hot and which are not. Formalizing those two processes and adding the remaining two components of counting and analyzing are all that's involved in starting an effective Trend-Watching system. It can take as little as a few minutes a day, without an elaborate staff or large budget. While some companies spend millions to get the right answers, the average businessperson cannot—and need not.

Simply put, Trend Watching is another way of keeping score—no less so than are statistics that track factory productivity, stock/price ratios, miles per gallon, or runs batted in. The "score," in this case, is a measure of what the public is learning, what it wants to know, and what it chooses to ignore.

News is the raw material of the Trend-Watching process, for reasons we'll explain later. In a broad sense, news media tell the public most of what it knows and acts on in relation to matters outside most people's immediate control. The media influence people on matters of politics, economics, and social behavior. This book explains how this process works, and shows you how to harness this information for your unique needs, using minimal time and expense.

The applications of Trend Watching are as varied as the needs of business itself. Firms large and small have used it to find new products and new markets that will meet changing conditions. Trend Watching is a way to gauge public relations, judge the competition, detect dangerous market conditions, predict elections, even analyze the suitability of stocks and other investments.

Good trend analysis is fairly simple. It focuses on hard information rather than subjective analysis. As it might have been for Coca-Cola, trend analysis can often be a reliable check on other, more elaborate means of measuring the market, finding new investment opportunities, understanding human relations, and coping with the whole range of problems every organization faces in dealing with the outside world.

Trend Watching provides a means for getting at those difficult questions that lie outside an organization and seem beyond its control. How will the public react to a new product? Will the services a company offers still be relevant in five years? What issues will employees be concerned about, and how might those issues affect business? Which markets will soon face downturns because of either changing needs or changing attitudes? What is the public's image of a particular industry?

There are endless examples of how Trend Watching can be used by organizations of almost any size. Consider the manager of a small plastics company. How does he deal with problems of waste disposal? What about his products in relation to child safety? Are there industry or government groups that can help him? What does he have in common with various advocacy groups? What about the image of different industry players in the community and in the nation?

Or consider the hardware-store owner facing the spring gardening season. What about pesticide sales? Which manufacturers have been in the news lately, locally or nationally? Are there alternatives to controversial products? What are the risks of stocking them—or of not stocking them?

You may be wondering what a business owner can learn from Trend Watching that he or she can't learn from customers or trade journals. Think about the possibilities from a business point of view. You may think that some of these questions are better answered by the "feel" of the market—who's buying what, for example. That means listening to signals from the customers themselves—an exercise for which there is no substitute—and keeping up on industry gossip, another useful tool. But there are important questions that go beyond what local contacts can tell you.

Consider the hardware-store owner. What is the impact of a pesticide plant disaster in India, such as the one that occurred in Bhopal in 1984? Can that affect local stores? It can if there is any identification between the distant disaster and the retail products, or if there is heightened fear of poisons in general. The consumer of gardening materials is also a consumer of national news, and his or her behavior may be conditioned by messages from far away.

Trend Watching is a relatively new art. You must probe deeply to find out where and how it is being used. Some companies, like Du Pont, may be as unaware of their trend-spotting systems as they are secretive. Many firms call their Trend-Watching techniques by other names, such as "environmental scanning," "issues management," or "emerging issues." A few lump those tasks into their planning departments.

Some of the most valuable trend analysis is almost unconscious. We all know someone—maybe ourselves—who reads everything, from *U.S. News & World Report* to the *Utne Reader*, and seems to have most things figured out. Trend Watching allows those of us who are somewhat less industrious to catch up, to make better use of the information we do consume and, most important, to assemble data that can be stored and manipulated to yield far more insight than those alleged geniuses who keep it all in their heads.

Please understand. Trend Watching is not a substitute for futures research, which looks at long-term change; or for market research, which attempts to show what groups of people are thinking. Properly used, however, Trend Watching is a support for these efforts, an insurance policy of sorts. But Trend Watching can also stand on its own as a quick and reliable way for business people with limited resources to understand what's going on around them.

The "Now" Society

Trend Watching begins with finding out where in the world of information you are now and where you are going. One of the curious realities of modern life is that we spend so much time doing this, with minimal results. The everyday demands of business and personal life leave most of us with precious little energy to focus on anything but the immediate present. Spending time looking into the future is a luxury few of us can afford.

Viewing the past with anything more than nostalgia or 20/20 hindsight can be an equally difficult, time-consuming task.

We have become a society "of the moment." To most of us, last year's news is as passé as high silk hats. If you doubt this, look through copies of last year's newspapers and news-magazines. You won't see fashions that are radically different or conclude that society or culture has made profound leaps. But you'll find that yesterday's news seems largely irrelevant today. News of Walter Mondale in 1984 or the Tylenol poisoning in 1982, important as they once were, has lost much of its impact.

It's hard enough to keep track of the present, let alone look into the past; the world is moving too fast. There's simply too much information, and it is easy to lose perspective. Most of us want to delegate the task of explaining things to our political and institutional leaders, the media, and the purveyors of "new technology," among others. Besides, there are other, more pressing matters: quarterly profits, hostile takeovers, keeping fit, the stock market, the kids, staying solvent. Determining long- and mid-term changes is part of that amorphous mass of unpleasant things in life we inevitably leave to someone else. But the value of trends is such that we can't leave this important task to someone else. As you will see, the implications of the Trend-Watching process on your business can be as varied as its applications. Among other benefits, you will be able to use trends to make predictions, manage the present, and assess public opinion and the media. Let's look at each of these.

1. Making Predictions

The value of forecasting is typically seen almost exclusively in foretelling the near future. The economics are very simple. If you know what the price of wheat will be tomorrow in Chicago, you can usually make a few dollars, perhaps a killing, in the wheat market. In larger terms, if you can predict market demand, you will know how to invest, how much raw materials to buy, when to sell off inventory, or how to set marketing strategy, among other things.

Trend analysis can give important clues to the mid-range future, too. It can tell a great deal about the direction people are headed in; about their anxieties and hopes; about what they are and aren't interested in; about their attitudes toward companies and other institutions, products, and people; and about what they are likely to be doing over the next few years. Trends are not absolute guides, but they can greatly improve the accuracy of your own estimates.

2. Managing the Present

Such prediction notwithstanding, the greatest value of Trend Watching may be in becoming more in touch with what is happening *today*. Predictions about the future, after all, are primarily educated extensions of the present. While such prognostications are always a bit chancy, there are few risks in and almost no limits to what you can learn about the here and now. Trend Watching can be a superb way to reduce data intake to a manageable flow and make useful calculations about the range of changes that affect you. One highly useful technique is, over time, to develop measurements of broader flows of information. Tracking such flows on a regular basis greatly increases your ability to gain perspective and to manage changes that are already upon you.

The trends we will watch are significantly different from those marked by historians as evidence of "changing times." Historians have one major advantage over Trend Watchers: They can look back. Hindsight is great stuff; you can always be sure that your methodology is up to date. Its weakness is that it is not contemporary. Historians can never see things as they really were. They must look at past events from the perspective of the time in which they write. In contrast, trends are contemporary history, written in contemporary thought, for future—and present—use.

3. Assessing Public Opinion and the Media

Trend Watching helps to put you and your organization's image into perspective with your markets and your competition.

By taking regular measurements of current information, you can remove the guesswork from media analysis and gain a more accurate picture of what the public is hearing. This is extremely important in an era in which history is less often seen as a series of events and is more often defined as the media's perception of the public's interpretation of those events. In this sense, "image"—once regarded as an intangible, the domain of public relations mavens—can become a very real asset or liability for both individuals and companies.

"Media trends" are the same in most respects as "societal trends"; the former merely describe the latter. Therefore, as you watch and understand trends, you are at the same time watching and understanding media. The link between media and trends has vastly changed the way people look at the world. The measurement of trends in media coverage has added a whole new dimension to the analysis of current events. (We shall discuss this linkage more thoroughly in Chapter Three.)

The Low Cost of Trend Watching

While the value of Trend Watching to your business endeavors is high, it may come as a surprise to you that the cost is low. As when gauging the value of most business activities, there are two considerations: time and money.

The typical person in business can devote little time to watching trends, a factor that leads an inordinate number of trend-conscious folks to turn to gurus and others who offer quick and dirty shortcuts. *Fortune* magazine, in a 1985 article* critical of the growing business of trend consultants, put it this way: "If you're a well-read person who listens to what's going on you probably don't need them." *Fortune* is probably right. If you are a well-read person, you have already taken a first step to becoming a Trend Watcher. What you need now is a system to make your consumption of that printed material as

* "Who Needs a Trend-Spotter," Myron Magnet (December 9, 1985), p. 56.

useful as possible, a system that will actually *save* you time. If you're not already a glutton for news, you should begin consuming selected publications in a fashion designed to get the most out of your valuable reading time.

There are few out-of-pocket costs involved in Trend Watching, aside from costs of the publications you will be (or already are) tracking. Indeed, a Trend-Watching program may actually save you money by limiting the publications you read to those absolutely essential for spotting trends. The bottom line is that your costs may be little more than what you are spending now on news and information materials, and possibly less.

Confidentiality in a Trend-Watching program is another vital consideration. The value of your insights increases if you keep them in house. You may very well not want to tip off your business plans, for example, by asking consultants or other outsiders sensitive questions about markets or products. The overall cost-effectiveness of Trend Watching lies in gaining a great deal of relevant information for your specific and confidential use, at very low cost. Elaborate systems are seldom necessary. The key elements are brain power and imagination. The real cost, therefore, is the time it takes to gain the discipline.

Three Case Studies

General Motors represents a good example of a large company in which Trend Watching techniques are used effectively. As it does with its research in many other areas, GM has gone at "societal research," as it calls it, in a rigorous fashion. A small unit at the GM Research Facility at Warren, Michigan, uses a wide range of external and internal data to answer not only questions about reactions to "wind noise" and consumer satisfaction, but a variety of international social questions as well. The team, under the direction of Dr. Walter A. Albers, Jr., is multidisciplinary. So are the information sources used, which range from media and trend data to survey research and other analytical processes. The goal is to see where society is going, in order that GM can build better products and better meet market demand. It is not a public affairs operation; it is an attempt to understand social change and to find useful answers for the operations team.

The GM operation was set up to look at a broad swatch of external information: social, technical, and political. As Albers, himself a physicist, says, "The real job is to integrate the materials, find out how they fit together, and then see what relates to GM concerns." Albers' unit seems to have the freedom to determine what it looks at and may propose for action. One of its unique features, vital for Trend Watching, is the quantification of data, enabling it to be integrated with data from other GM departments. In this way, GM's Societal Research Department can talk on a par with its peers in operations. One of the unit's successes has been advocacy since the mid-1970s, both inside and outside of GM, of seat belts as a safety device. GM has been highly innovative in encouraging the use of belts, and its campaign has paid off both in terms of greater public safety and in avoiding the cost of more expensive regulation.

Another Trend-Watching model can be found at the Monsanto Company, which has been a pioneer in effective "proactive" public relations in an industry beset by major problems and crises. Monsanto has used an intensive external and internal scan to break issues down into categories by time and appearance. Their analysis has been used to assess problems from a variety of perspectives, ranging from how responsible to society the company should be to how it can organize its business objectives. These are functions of long-range studies. In addition, the current-issues group focuses on problems the company has an opportunity to influence over the next two years. Says Frank Stokes, former director of Issues Analysis in Monsanto's Public Affairs Department, "The major problem for big companies is not spotting new issues so much as keeping track and assigning priorities."

In a hot spot like the chemical industry, problems are often so big they can't be missed, but they are also so big they can't easily be put into perspective. Two examples cited as crucial for the years ahead are treatment of intellectual property, including international protection of patents, and regulation of biotechnology. In 1985, these were two of the current issues on a short list of priorities, boiled down from a much longer list of problems.

Monsanto represents the classic case of a company monitoring external problems on a continuing basis. Its focus is on issues, as opposed to operational change. It adjusts its focus according to the time frame of each issue, and seeks to fit each issue into the appropriate slot in the corporate structure, which results in a large part of the company being involved and responsive to changing situations.

Many of the examples in this book involve the chemical industry because it has been the focus of media and political attention so often that many of its member firms have become highly tuned to the outside world. We mentioned Du Pont earlier, the paragon that unconsciously seems to do things right because, as its loyal staffers claim, it has its heart in the right place. But it is important to keep its situation in perspective; Du Pont's achievements haven't been gained without much thought and expense.

Not surprisingly, the Chemical Manufacturers Association (CMA), the trade association that brings together the whole chemical industry, has developed its own unique and often-praised system for scanning issues. CMA's focus is strictly on the Washington scene, and on legislation affecting the industry. To broaden its perspective CMA relies on the scanning efforts of some 2,000 people from member organizations, who participate in a total of 2,000 or so task force meetings each year. Included in this scheme are a dozen standing committees on broad issues such as health and safety or environmental management, and whose meetings are open to all members. In this way, there is a broad cross-pollination of information coming from communities, plant sites, and public and government relations staff at all levels. CMA estimates that it takes an issue a full ten years to work its way through Congress. Some issues, like the industry's Superfund, are seen as perennial.

The focus of CMA's effort is advocacy. Its budget is organized by issue, so members can see how priorities are drawn. According to CMA communications chief Jon Holtzman, the key is timing: "If we can be two years ahead of the curve, we'll be 1.75 years ahead of everyone else." CMA's work in negotiating agreements on legislation and in setting up crisis management systems is one of the best working examples of the art of issues management.

These three systems—General Motors, Monsanto, and CMA—while involving widely different approaches, represent three good examples of the value of tracking, quantifying, and analyzing trend data. In the pages that follow, we will introduce the theory behind these systems, and describe the process of establishing your own Trend-Watching system—whether you're a prospective entrepreneur looking for a market niche to fill or the CEO of a multimillion dollar operation.

2
Information as a Moving Force

In an open society like ours, people's demand for information and their ability to gain access to it have created a whole new kind of body politic: the information democracy. We have committed ourselves to the fullest utilization of and freest access to knowledge. Consider some of the most difficult issues to resolve: limiting the photocopying of copyrighted material, preventing the illegal copying of software and videocassettes, and controlling the unauthorized use of television signals by owners of satellite dish receivers. These issues result from our high level of access to information.

For anyone to keep up with all the available information is next to impossible. Information is not static. It doesn't just exist; it moves. New data are added to old; information changes from one day to the next. We call these movements "information flows," reflecting the role of information as an active agent in society. The question, then, is whether it is possible to read these flows. Is there a way to look at the information flows so they will tell you about a change without your having to examine each separate piece of information? The answer is yes, if you can find patterns in the information flows themselves.

Trend Watching enables you to use "information about information" to keep pace with society in a new age.

What we value most about communication is the unpredictable, the smoke signal that tells us change is in the wind. Indeed, this is exactly what "news" is: those events or trends that could not be predicted, whether they are next year's inflation figures or tomorrow's grisly murder. As any journalism graduate can tell you, the bane of a news editor's existence is "dog bites man" stories—tales of everyday occurrences that surprise no one.

If the issue is whether country Y will invade country Z, or whether Congress will pass a new bill, the first thing to do in tracking a trend is to look for signs of departure from the norm that suggest something unpredictable is about to happen.

Let's take an example close to home. In 1986, the U.S. Senate took up a tax reform bill that had passed the House of Representatives months earlier. For many years, Congress had struggled with the complex provisions of such bills, and the tendency was to develop a bill full of exceptions, concessions, and various other loopholes favoring special interests. The rules of the Senate allow open amendment procedures—any senator can offer an amendment to a bill as it is debated on the Senate floor—and the customs of courtesy assure that no matter how trivial the cause, every member has an opportunity to serve his or her constituents.

The probability in this instance was that the Senate would produce a bill chock full of loopholes, swerves, and dodges; in early 1986, it began to do just that. The proposals hardly amounted to tax reform, scarcely even tax simplification. Then, improbably, Senate Finance Committee Chairman Bob Packwood of Oregon launched a successful initiative to sweep aside a host of loopholes, producing a new bill much more in keeping with the original aims of the legislation. It subsequently passed the Senate and, after relatively few compromises, became law.

Should we have been surprised? Were there any early "smoke signals" telling us things we didn't expect would happen? Yes. A year earlier, the national media had begun informing us of two things: (1) that tax reform was a positive idea and (2) that it had priority over other issues. The first message came from the substantive content of all major media messages, and the second developed from a sharp increase in public attention. Tax reform was the only domestic issue (aside from a brief flurry of interest about balancing the budget) that received more than 10 percent of all national news coverage in a period we measured during 1985. A reading of the information flows told us there was smoke someplace, and that fire was inevitable. The message was going out to the public and, presumably, coming back to Congress from its constituents: "Tax reform is good, so pass it."

How do we know this? When asked why he had altered his bill, Bob Packwood said that he kept hearing from fellow senators that they "wished they could vote for 'real' reform." The senators had read the messages of their constituents. They heard that tax reform was good and, being shrewd political animals, they knew their constituents had heard it as well.

Why tell this story? Because it makes two key points:

- It shows the power of messages sent via news media to the public to provoke a future response.
- It demonstrates the importance of spotting the flag of improbability in human conduct.

Both points are fundamental to understanding and harnessing the power of Trend Watching.

Packwood's comment came late in the day, but it was the key signal for immediately impending change. Had Packwood and the rest of Congress not moved toward tax reform, it likely would have happened anyway, but certainly not as quickly. Public pressure was building, and the message had become clear: Failure to pass tax reform would put the members up to scorn in an election year. Packwood read the signals, and— as is so often the case—he who reads the signals is often the best messenger, because he understands the information forces at work.

The Power of Information in Society

The technical definition of *information* stresses its power. Dictionary definitions say that information is essentially static, that it is: "Communication or reception of knowledge or intelligence"—that is, dull facts exchanged between files in a storage cabinet or one's brain. Today's definition by scientists and engineers concerned with electronic communications has begun to revive the active character of information as an agent in its own right. The engineering definition focuses on how electronic signals activate or deactivate mechanisms, convert electron flows into message units, or move data along a wire.

As we have labored in recent years to construct computerized analogues to our own gray matter, we have observed the human brain with increasing insight. Conversely, we have begun to think of our brains as computers, or even to view society as having a social sense based on a vast number of highly efficient information processors. There is very little in our daily life anymore that works purely on instinct. External information drives us from wakeup to bedtime—whether it be prices, laws, markets, forecasts, warnings, and, of course, "the news"—and keeps us mentally active in nighttime dreams.

It may be a crude analogue to suggest that society behaves as one great collective information processing system. That is certainly not the case. But when society receives information en masse and communicates in a social sense—in the marketplace or the voting booth, for example—the parallels can be drawn. As is often the case, the easiest comparisons involve political behavior. Consider an American presidential election. During its course, the public receives information over a set period of time known as a "campaign". Everyone registers an opinion simultaneously on Election Day. And the election behavior, therefore, provides a pretty good test of how the public messaging system works.

If media information passed on during a political campaign has power, it should affect, if not determine, the outcome, leaving aside any predispositions voters may have had to start with.

Let's look at an example of this. In 1984, the Democratic party put together a slate of candidates, all of whom, including a former vice president, were marginally known or approved of by the public. During the three months of primary campaigning, the national media changed their view of the two principal contenders, Senator Gary Hart and Vice President Walter Mondale, at three distinct points in time, with both positive and negative coverage of Mondale and Hart. Directly following each of these shifts in media favor, the results in state primaries conformed with the media's most recent message. If coverage of Mondale's negatives was down and his other coverage was large enough to overcome their drag, he would win the primary—providing Hart's coverage hadn't followed a similar pattern.

Figure 2-1 illustrates how the national media function as a predictor. The graph shows composite media ratings for the 1984 Democratic primaries. The various primaries are shown by vertical breaks in the graph, positioned according to the time between March and July when they were held. The media ratings are shown on the vertical axis, and represent a quantification of gains and losses in image.

As the figure shows, media coverage of Mondale rose from a negative following the New Hampshire primary in February 1984, to a positive peak by mid-April. On the other hand, Hart sank quickly after the New Hampshire primary, because he had to fend off questions about such matters as his real age and name, but he recovered before the Ohio primary in May; whereas Mondale had again sagged by this time, having gotten all he could squeeze out of his "Where's the Beef?" comment. By the end of the primary season, the media were careful to draw less distinction between candidates and, not surprisingly, the election outcomes were closer.

Negative media messages saying "don't vote for this guy" were found to have a decisive effect throughout the campaign. In Figure 2-1, negative coverage was weighted 4 to 1 over other coverage. On successive occasions, negative messages in na-

Figure 2-1 National media coverage for candidates in 1984 Democratic primaries.

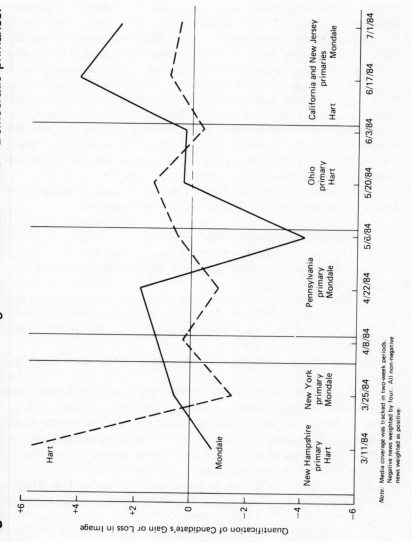

Note: Media coverage was tracked in two-week periods.
Negative news weighted by four. All non-negative
news weighted as positive.

tional media coverage were decisive for each candidate's chances. Through Trend Watching—in this case, monitoring the national media—it was possible to predict nearly all the election results several days in advance. It should be noted that the winner of a primary always had better national media coverage, except in California. There, the voters listened to their state's voices rather than the national media. (The California exception is instructive. The *Los Angeles Times*, for example, liked Senator Hart a lot more than did the Eastern media and, being closer to its audience, the *L.A. Times'* voice was heard. In Trend Watching, it is always important to understand which media messages really count.)

This example provides a good basis for understanding how Trend Watching works. There are six key points:

1. Voters must make a decision.
2. The decision-making period is a fixed time.
3. There are a limited number of ways information can reach voters.
4. Almost all key information finds its way into election coverage, reaching the public through a media filter.
5. It is relatively easy to distinguish between positive and negative coverage.
6. Data can be quantified to show gains and losses in image.

The example of the 1984 Democratic primary shows how information filtering through society can affect public choice. We will return to this example later to explain more about prediction. For now, it's important to appreciate the role of information as an agent and, hence, as a maker of trends.

In 1984, the voters responded in near-virtual lockstep with the images that the media painted of the candidates. This is not always the case, and there are other factors that must be considered. Still, the striking relationship between the flow of media messages to the public prior to election and the successive electoral outcomes illustrates our point: Information power is the force that messages exert on the public mind, leading to later action.

Watching Media Flows

Economic behavior has long been the subject of profitable trend analysis based on mathematical projection. The study of economics is blessed with two advantages: It aims to help create wealth, and it has been reduced to numbers. No other social science has been so thoroughly quantified and prepared for an era of high-speed information. Since John Stuart Mill's invention of the demand and supply curves as the "calculus of pleasure and pain," economists have been Trend Watchers.

The use of charts in the stock market is an example of a type of Trend Watching behavior. The chartist looks for signals suggesting that the direction of a stock—or of the market as a whole—will change. An arsenal of methods are devised to spot these signals. Essentially, all relate to the state of supply and demand as understood by those in the market.

Sometimes the charts themselves have an effect as they "inform," activating brokers to buy or sell. It seems like classic information age behavior: codes and active information controlling large movements of materials or money far removed from the scene of action. But this is not *true* Trend Watching. The chartists rely on history repeating itself—on certain stock/price cycles being predictable. And, unlike most other forms of Trend Watching, chart analysis is based on information after the fact rather than before.

Economists have suffered in recent years at the hands of critics who claim they have failed to predict change correctly. From our point of view, one reason for this criticism is obvious. Economics, though based on "hard" data, does not always make use of information as an agent of change. It uses data as artifacts of past events, without looking at the effects of information on public behavior. Extrapolating these artifacts often leads to trouble. Economists have been most effective when they use economic data as a signal of future public behavior, as in the case of demand and supply curves.

Sometimes the use of numbers, regardless of origin, becomes so engrossing that it leads to a misreading of history. In his biographies of early economists, Robert Heilbroner writes of Francis Ysidro Edgeworth, who tried to reduce all economic knowledge to equations. His expression for Ireland's 1848 Potato Famine was written:

$$\frac{d_2y}{dx^2} = \frac{\left(\frac{d\pi}{dx}\right)^2 \left(\frac{d_2\pi}{dy^2}\right) - 2\frac{d\pi d\pi}{\partial x \partial y}\left(\frac{\partial_2\pi}{\partial x \partial y}\right) + \left(\frac{\partial\pi}{\partial y}\right)^2 \left(\frac{\partial_2\pi}{\partial x^2}\right)}{-\left(\frac{d\pi}{\partial y}\right)^3}$$

Accurate, perhaps, but there's not much there to use to prevent further potato famines—or any other kind of famine, for that matter. Edgeworth's equation, like the work of many macroeconomists since, had the classic defect of not accounting for the impact of information on people and how they would react to it. It was assumed that people would behave in certain ways in their own self-interest—that they were suffering from a widespread famine, for example, and that only a concerted effort would save the day. People did, in fact, behave as expected, but only when they had adequate information about where their self-interests lay. Many Irish farmers had no idea of what was happening, nor, in fact, did English officialdom, which lacked meaningful data. Many are the stories of superstition and distrust, even outright ignorance, that come from such times of mass crisis.

What's needed for today's economists and other forecasters is a better sense of how the thought processes of the public work. Businesses seek to fill this need by survey research, but the process is often costly and voluminous. There isn't time to survey all the questions a businessperson needs to know about economic behavior, even granting that certain economic theories hold true. But there certainly is time for an interested individual to develop a useful world view from these data.

The high-speed information age requires something both simpler and faster: simpler, by virtue of being easily understood as part of a larger system; faster, because there just isn't time to ask every potential customer what fully is on his or her mind. The answer is to use information *about* information. This is the essence of Trend Watching. There simply is no better way to deal with the complexities of our modern economy and yet develop an individualized, entrepreneurial approach to it.

For every imaginable subject, it is possible to graph movements of information flows to the public at large, or within a given sector of the population. You can use these graphs to determine the kind of information entering the public's collective mind on political issues, key aspects of market behavior, social attitudes, and a variety of other topics. This system not only provides a more rapid view, but also a more accurate one.

Let's examine media coverage of interest rates, for example. Covering the period from the first quarter of 1984 through the first half of 1986, Figure 2-2 illustrates how two different scales can be used to plot the same type of activity. One scale (right-hand) simply shows the changes in interest rates; the other (left-hand) tracks the number of media messages received by the public that accompanied those changes. Note that changes in interest rates did not always generate the same public reaction or level of concern. As interest rates declined through most of 1984 and all of 1985, for example, media decreased its attention. This was during an era in which economic news was relatively positive. However, between the fourth quarter of 1985 and the first quarter of 1986, declines in interest rates suddenly became bigger news as the media began to signal that the economy was slowing down and needed help. But interest rates were only part of the picture. News about all aspects of money, including Federal Reserve actions, stock exchange activity, bank failures, and other issues signaled a much earlier concern for the economy by rising sharply in mid-1985 and continuing into 1986. This was an early signal that the economy was slowing down.

The three lines together—media coverage of interest rates, media coverage of all money issues, and the Federal Reserve discount rate—tell us a great deal more about potential public reaction to future changes than looking at interest rates alone. By including the media data, we can get an idea of how information is at work on the public's mind. It shows that

Figure 2-2 National media coverage of money issues, compared with federal discount rate.

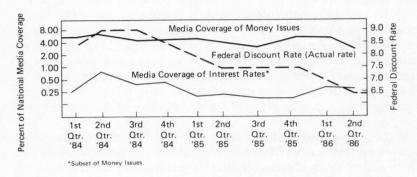

*Subset of Money Issues.

public concern about the downturn in the economy appeared quite strongly in the last half of 1985 and early 1986.

The information age offers a new dimension to economics and to economic Trend Watching. Because economics is already concerned with trends, it is relatively simple to devise time-specific questions about economic change and apply knowledge of trends to help see into the future.

Social Trend Watching

Trends in social behavior have often been called "fads." People are called "trendy" if they buy the right clothes, eat the right ice cream, or play the right sports. Trends of this kind are usually imitative, depending on information only in its simplest form.

We are not interested in fads. We are interested in informed social movements, in actions that gather strength in society and change its course. In earlier times, movements might evolve in different places at the same time because the paths of history in each place somehow led to parallel developments. In our modern world, coincidental actions without communication among the actors is far less common. People seek out a common ground with others who have the same concerns. They search for support and avoid adversaries. Trends now develop around informed actions—a relatively simple process in today's global village, in which the lives of any person, from Rock Hudson to Desmond Tutu, can become the focus of instant international intrigue through a relative handful of well-placed media reports.

But what about true pace-setting social trends and issues of mores and priorities, from child-rearing to church-going, from medicine to marriage? People do follow leaders who set appropriate examples and who communicate to them. This is not the same as slavish imitation, however. Leadership involves informing people, often through training and education, and also by seeking support based on informed opinion, usually through the print and broadcast media. Without media reports, for example, we would not be aware that AIDS has dramatically changed people's dating patterns; those very reports, in fact, ensure that the changes become even more dramatic and long-lasting.

In today's America, social change can take place very fast. The complex forming—and dismantling—of institutions takes place hand in hand with the surge in opinion and action. Today's religious or political leaders can be tomorrow's scandalized victims, as media revelations tear apart what seemed to be rock-solid certainties. The extent to which this change takes place is in direct relationship to media coverage, whether it is intensive coverage spanning a few days or slow, steady, and persistent coverage over months or years. In either case, the more information that penetrates the public mind, the greater its effect will be.

Especially with regard to social behavior, information is retained in the public memory, to reappear powerfully at later times. Both the media and the public retain strong views for many years on problems posed by disasters, scandals, and other topics of heavy media coverage. Because of herpes and AIDS, for example, it will take years, if it happens at all, before dating practices revert to the casual sex of the 1960s' Sexual Revolution. In a few short months, centuries of sexual taboos that had gradually been overcome have now reappeared, albeit not to the same degree of intensity. As news of sexually transmitted diseases reached each new revelation or crossed some dreaded new threshhold (that presence of the AIDS virus was increasing among heterosexual women, for example), the social entrenchment increased in lockstep.

This retained information has to do with the notion of "public memory," a concept based on some biologists' belief that memory is never really lost. The retention time, they say, is at least proportional to the measure of exposure to the initial event. The intensity of crises produces a strong public memory and generates a watchful media surveillance for new developments. In turn, these new developments generate a stronger public memory and more media surveillance. And on and on, until it becomes so commonplace—so much a part of our consciousness—that it no longer is "news." It becomes the proverbial "dog bites man" story. Fortunately for Trend Watchers, each development is fairly easy to track and to assess for future scenarios.

Media Trendsetters

When developments have not yet warranted substantial mass media coverage, specialized periodicals often herald new movements. The weekly publication of the prestigious *New England Journal of Medicine*, for example, is often so worthy of attention that stories based on its articles are immediately picked up by wire services, networks, and other mass media. This is a standard technique of Trend Watching: Watch the trendsetters— the key research publications like the *New England Journal of Medicine*—or follow the elite groups or networks. We'll describe this further in Chapter Six. The point here is that, increasingly in the information age, what is important is picked up and described by reporters in one form or another. By setting up suitable systems of scanning publications, even obscure ones, you can discern the first signs of movement.

Networking is another way in which specialized information travels. The network is a unique creation of our time. It is nothing more than a group of people with common interests, who work together for reinforcement and for exchange of ideas. Networks tend to develop their own communications schemes, often in the form of newsletters whose information is so precise and so highly focused that they can command high prices. Tapping into the right newsletter can be an efficient way to bring to light a spate of clues on trends within small sectors.

There also tends to be an elitism about trends as we have described them so far: People with ideas influence others who are smart enough to use those ideas. Trend analysis will always be skewed toward the more intelligent, if only because these people are social leaders. Yet the system isn't necessarily limited to the elite. Trends also work their way through society by an aggregation of actions. In a country the size of the United States, a certain amount of what seems to be spontaneous generation of trends can occur. This may be ascribed to coincidence, but more often it happens when different groups of people react to the same situation in similar ways. In the argot of the information age, we'd say that each group is reacting not to a situation, but to what it knows about it, and that those in the groups have all come to the same conclusions.

Thus it is often possible to measure a series of events and spot a trend without looking directly at the information flows involved. This is especially so when dealing with social trends—those significant events involving people, not natural disasters or the weather. Social trends often appear as a series of people acting in increasingly common ways, whether it is marketplace behavior or changes in dating habits.

Unfortunately, these significant events involving people—social trends—become news. It is possible, then, to track news coverage about these events in local communities. For example, if several cities and states are found to adopt the "social contract" concept of setting utility rates, the presumption is that the trend will begin to spread from these bellweathers throughout the country. The assumption that what starts at the grass-roots level can spread nationwide is at the heart of the trend-spotting technique favored by some corporate issues managers and is also that used by John Naisbitt in his landmark book *Megatrends.*

Trend Watching vs. Megatrends

The big difference between John Naisbitt's technique and Trend Watching is that Naisbitt's method involves simply counting and measuring the number of times an event occurs and is reported in local media. As the number of similar incidents increases, a trend can be seen to be spreading. It places events against a calendar or against a geographical spread.

Our Trend Watching system takes this process one step further. Like Naisbitt, we count the number of events, but we also count how much attention each event receives—what we call the Index of Exposure—and, therefore, how people are likely to react to that exposure. Naisbitt measures local newspapers to find things others haven't yet seen and to spot movements based on the number of different times something recurs around the country. This is a valid forecasting tool. But we take this process one step further by calculating not just the number of articles on a given subject, but how much attention those issues receive. In other words, while *Megatrends* counts the *number of articles* about an issue, Trend Watching measures the total *volume of coverage* the media chooses to give that issue.

The volume of coverage is measured in terms of column-inches or broadcast-minutes. For example, if stories about a given topic appear a specific number of times in newspapers and on television news programs around the country, that is important to know, especially if the number of occurrences is increasing or decreasing over time. If you know that the total volume of coverage on that topic has changed over time, you have a much clearer picture of what the public is learning.

Let's look at the issue of limiting jury awards in malpractice suits. Suppose, for example, that articles reporting the views of those supporting award limits appeared in 75 newspapers, while articles reporting the views of those against award limits appeared in 50 papers. (We'll leave television out of this for matters of simplicity.) That's interesting to know. It would appear that support for limiting jury awards was getting more press. But what happens when we measure exposure? We might find that while the 75 stories favoring limits were spread over 1,000 column-inches, the 50 stories about the opponents received 3,000 column-inches. Thus a smaller number of articles generated a considerably larger volume of coverage.

When you factor in the likelihood that greater press coverage will be picked up by other media—television networks, for example, and perhaps a major newsweekly—it vastly increases the story's impact on the public mind. In part, this is because in-depth stories provide more grist for other reporters' mills, giving them more detail and other resources with which to pursue additional stories. It also gives the public more grounds on which to act, whether in a referendum or in the marketplace. It is a story's exposure, not the mere presence of a story, that makes information an active agent.

Watching What *Doesn't* Happen

Another key aspect of Trend Watching is recognizing what *isn't* being covered. If information doesn't move among potential actors, action won't happen. Thus, lack of coverage can be an important factor, too. It occurs most often through de-emphasis or a reduced flow of data rather than through intentional concealment or "disinformation."

Take international news, for example. In the mid 1980s, international events assumed an increasing proportion of national news capacity, moving from 30 percent in 1982 to 50 percent in 1986. As a consequence, there has been less print space and airtime to cover domestic issues. Environmental coverage, for example, has dropped dramatically. (Between 1982 and 1986, environmental coverage dropped 30 percent, from just over 2 percent in 1982 to 1.4 percent in 1986.) Decreased media attention, in turn, has gone hand in hand with decreased support for leading environmental organizations and less public demand for regulation.

You can easily think of a number of cases in which interest in new ideas or problems has driven out concern for—and therefore information about—other ideas or problems. How many times have you seen press campaigns by corporations or political candidates that have been designed to focus attention away from embarrassing issues? For example, advertisements for breakfast cereals often stress delicious "fruit" instead of healthful but tasteless fiber; in a mud-slinging political campaign, candidates' personal dirty laundry becomes a bigger campaign issue than the economic and social problems of everyday life.

The idea is simple. When considering the major national media, remember that there is a relatively stable number of column-inches and broadcast-minutes. When coverage of some topic increases, coverage of another topic must decrease. News editors abhor a vacuum, and in the information age, there is never a shortage of data to fill a void.

As any politician seeking name recognition can attest, a subject requires a great deal of communication before a large portion of the population hears it, and hears it right. So it is important to have some gauge of transmission volume over a period of time to understand how deeply an idea may be penetrating, or not penetrating. As mentioned previously, in Trend Watching we call this the Index of Exposure. For single bursts of news, there seems to be a threshhold at somewhere around 10 percent of total national news capacity; that is, one-tenth of all column-inches or broadcast-minutes for a given period. If at any time an event or issue gets this much coverage, you can reliably assume that the public has heard the story and will remember at least the bare essentials. Stories that reach a lot of people—disasters and tragic deaths of famous people, for example—generally are retained in the public memory for a longer period of time.

A cumulative feeding of small amounts of information does not have as strong an effect as the sudden impact of a story that reaches the public all at once. This is in large part because the blockbuster news item is almost always a disaster or other type of negative story, while persistent smaller stories often can contain positive as well as negative elements. For example, years of reinforcing confidence in over-the-counter capsule medicine at a fairly low order of magnitude couldn't compensate for the explosive 1982 news coverage of the first Tylenol tampering. Even though the product regained its market, it could not hold out in 1985, when a relatively small second story triggered the public's memory of earlier news that had once spread widely across the country. Johnson & Johnson, Tylenol's maker, felt obliged to get out of the capsule business. Smaller levels of news transmission seem to reach chiefly the literate, the interested, and the influential. Blockbuster stories reach everybody.

Much social communication is antidemocratic. Our society is rigged with systems that ensure good communication among intelligent, educated people. This communication is often direct: one to one and carefully targeted. Communication to the broad public, however, rests on scattershot methods and random chance, which increase the likelihood that a message won't get through to everybody. In a national news system, the quality of information deteriorates extremely quickly.

Measuring Information Means Measuring Trends

Let's summarize the major points in this chapter:

- Information is a major agent of change and movement in modern society, particularly in the United States.
- This movement and change can be understood by scanning the flows of information causing that change.
- Scanning information flows can be simplified by learning how to read their distinguishing characteristics.
- Trends can be measured by reading and measuring information flows.

The balance of this book is devoted to a further understanding of the media and to setting up an effective Trend Watching program for the least cost in time and money.

3

Why Use News?

When we seek out data for Trend Watching, we must find information with specific qualities: It must be able to move large numbers of people, be easily accessible to these people, and be in demand. We're not interested in high-priced secrets or in what some researcher is saying, unless we know that the researcher's abstruse work will eventually reach the masses.

In general, we must avoid information that has little use to its recipients. For example, a Trend-Watching data base developed from self-serving press releases would contain very little informational power because the recipients of those releases would have heavily discounted or ignored most of the information.

Moreover, there must be some tangible value to the information, lest there be no reason for people to want it, let alone use it. In other words, there must be some cost for receiving the information. But not much cost; people's willingness to pay the "price" of putting up with television ads, for example, is rather low.

As a Trend Watcher, you don't want to exclude any part of the public from your surveys. What you are looking for is the largest volume of information available to the public, and for which the public is willing to pay, in terms of dollars or time.

Almost by definition, we are talking about daily news. News is the common denominator for information in our society. It is the information source, more than any other, that defines and moves society. It is the means by which people act in a social way, be it by voting, buying, selling, or avoiding bad weather. News is the mass information that Trend Watchers must use to read the information flows in American society.

One of the characteristics of news is that it has little force unless it is held in common. Almost consciously, people seek out news sources that they know others are using. The television newscast that gets the higher ratings will soon get even higher ratings. There is a herding effect in news watching. Developments are "news" because they are what everyone needs to know and is believed to know.

That's what makes news a principal information agent. We begin Trend Watching with this body of messages because everyone receives them. In the United States, this means at the outset that a relatively small group of media control the national news. We know that, to a greater or lesser extent, all society is somehow motivated by this general news. As you become increasingly sophisticated in Trend Watching, you may add more specialized media to give an additional dimension to your measurements and gain much enhanced value.

Trend Watching begins with news—what everyone knows—and then moves toward specific concerns. No other approach is fully logical. You must start with the premise that you want to know what the public knows. You can't look for partial knowledge until you have the broader picture. Even if you are interested solely in the behavior of metallurgists, for example, or dancers or advertising buyers, you still must know what information is influencing them. Ad buyers may be following the progress of new presentation techniques, but like everyone else, they learn from the national news of the concerns people have about such things as automobile safety, water pollution, or nutrition.

The United States offers special advantages to Trend Watchers. The news that is available here largely represents the news people want, as expressed by their purchases or patronage of newspapers, magazines, and newscasts. In some other countries, propaganda often interferes with the news system. In such cases, the forces of information may not be altogether lost, but the effect of any given piece of information is usually skewed by the reaction of a wise public: "Oh, that's the politburo again." Or, "That's what the Presidential Palace wants us to believe."

Reactions are much more difficult to discern if the news audience suspects a motive in the source of news reporting. In the United States, the public is often aware of the "spin" given a story by a government official or publicist. Even here, we sometimes have difficulties with the filtering system through which information passes as it moves to the public. But our problems are small compared to other countries. In this country, there is a free and open market for ideas and information that, in the long run, operates against biases and in favor of accurate reporting.

Bias in the Daily Mirror

The media are the daily mirrors of people's activities. They reflect society's deeds and thoughts. The ideal of a truly objective press doesn't exist, of course. There are reporters' biases, newsroom agendas, indifference to some issues, prejudice against others, and just plain blind spots. Much of this is the result of a tendency for all parts of the media to write the same story on the same day. Much like their readers, journalists herd naturally, too.

But the distortion that develops between an actual public action, its reflection in the media, and its ultimate perception by the public has much more to do, in America, with the way the media work as business organizations than with spin or bias. For instance, many business people outside the media find it hard to accept that, by and large, America's media seek to present the public with what it needs and wants to hear. Media are businesses—not like any other, but businesses nonetheless. Ultimately, they depend on the goodwill and support of their "customers"—their readers, viewers, and advertisers.

Any other interpretation of the media's role, especially a con-
spiratorial one that looks upon them as controlled by one group
or another, will founder when trying to show how bias is
consistent throughout the system.

Fortunately, America has a large and diverse assortment
of media that enable Trend Watchers to factor out specific
biases. There are major papers with liberal policies and others
with conservative ones. As it should in a free-market society,
the market sets limits to the biases; there is no strong media
representation of the socialist Left, for example, because there
doesn't seem to be a market for it. And within the market's
imposed limits, one bias balances another. Because Trend
Watching chiefly involves an overview of a large pool of information, you can come pretty close to getting the "average
public opinion" by tracking a cross-section of relatively few
major news media.

Reporters change their views based on public opinion, too.
This can be demonstrated by measuring the coverage given to
partisan issues over a period of time to see how it compares
with preferences expressed at the ballot box. Following is a
table showing coverage of key liberal issues at early and later
stages of the Reagan administration. The media's move to the
right is clear; as the electorate became more conservative, so
did the media coverage.

National Media Coverage of "Liberal" Issues 1983–86
(percent of total media coverage)

	1983	1984	1985	1986
Environmental issues	2.2	2.1	1.8	1.3
"Fairness" issues	3.8	3.3	2.7	2.1
Reagan Administration (criticism)	3.8	2.7	1.4	1.2
Arms control	2.4	1.3	2.5	1.1

As you can see, in each category the amount of coverage declined over the four-year period. In other words, the media read the election returns and responded according to "the market," giving the electorate a mix of stories with increasingly less coverage of these "liberal" issues.

But even if the bias problem is eliminated by averaging the media coverage and by periodically checking the drift of major publications, Trend Watchers may still have a problem with the way the daily mirror reflects a day's events back to the public. Getting the bias problem out of the way only helps you see the problem more directly in terms of how information moves.

The Circular Flow

The images people get from the media are reflections of what is taking place. Because media, too, are looking at a vast range of information sources, they must filter out a lot of data to determine what is truly worth covering. Definitions at this point become circular: News is what the media choose to make news.

On a daily basis, that's the way it works. In the longer run, if a news organization makes a series of bad choices—if it somehow misreads "the market"—it fails, gets reorganized, or is otherwise shaken up. There is a reward for the media that consistently make the right choices: success. The result is a public that is supplied fairly consistently with the mix of information it wants, even if a few biases manage to survive.

Looking at the media as marketers of news, we see that there must be a flow of information from the public back to the media, just as news flows the other way. The public provides the media with two valuable things:

- The public is the media's source of information for the news they produce. News, in the broadest sense, is about the public: it is people, their actions, and their institutions.
- The public tells media managers what it is interested in. In this sense the media's own reporters and editors are

Figure 3-1 The continuous flow of news to and from the media.

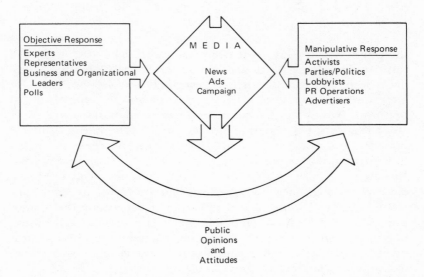

Public
Opinions
and
Attitudes

the link in the marketing chain. A "good story" is one people need to know and want to read.

Figure 3-1 represents how the news flow operates. Note that while the media distribute news to the public in a single stream, there are two ways the media take news from the public.

The News Market

Most professional journalists aren't happy with the notion that they are market researchers; but to an extent that is what they are. While such an identity may place them in a class somewhat below the level of movers and shakers, journalists are nonetheless essential to the making of trends, and the market-research function remains very much a part of their daily job. In perhaps no other industry is the relationship between the supply of the product and the maintenance of its demand so closely related. After all, what other product provides its customers with a forum for daily feedback in the form of letters to the editor?

The service provided by the media can be seen as giving the public what it knows it needs. News isn't news if it doesn't tell people something valuable. Very often it is something they don't want to hear: that it is increasingly less safe to travel by airplane, that the risk of AIDS is also high among heterosexuals, or that this may be the coldest winter in memory.

News tends to operate on the same principle as the oil light on your car's dashboard. The light has no real use unless it comes on, indicating your engine is down a couple of quarts. In news, the information about which the public has the most clearly defined need to know is that involving trouble—an improbability of something happening, an indication that something is wrong, or a notice that something is changing. An ideal newspaper, in fact, would be one that accurately gives all the clues to change, all the improbabilities, everything people need to know to anticipate what lies ahead.

Information flows from the public reach media organizations in two different ways. Reporters and editors prefer, above all, to seek out information themselves. Such information is regarded as more valuable and reliable. It is trusted because it comes with fewer built-in biases, and it is the media's own product—not the result of a news conference by someone with a story to tell—with the concomitant pride of "ownership." There is no higher prize in the newsroom than a scoop.

As reporters fan out over their beats, they are in contact with their sources, who are also part of their readership. Every newsroom has a daily input of information about public action and reaction. It is the media's job to keep on top of all this, and more.

Increasingly, much of this information about the public's state of knowledge and mind is specifically geared for determining that very purpose. It is no accident that major media are linked with polling operations—the CBS/New York Times poll, for example. Reporters want to know what the public is thinking, which in turn becomes grist for their editorial mills. Outwardly, such polls are news, but they are also clues to the demand for more news.

The newsroom is, therefore, a kind of news market. Stories rise and fall on the basis of the collective wisdom of the staff and the decisions of editors. Ultimately, it is the editors who make the final judgments about what is "news," about what the public needs and wants to know, about what reporting constitutes a genuine public service and what is dross. It is the editors, then, who decide what America learns. Their guideposts include the standards of journalism, their own judgments, and the arguments of their colleagues. They also have an abiding concern for the continuing existence and prosperity of the institutions they serve.

To liken the news process entirely to a marketplace may be carrying the analogy too far. There are several important differences. For one thing, journalists and editors enjoy what they do and are generally less motivated than people in other fields by commercial gain. They are not really involved in sales, and the marketing aspect of their job is more subtle. What they are selling is "all the news that's fit to print," as the *New York Times* puts it. Editors are meeting a voracious demand to know about daily life. Their problem, like the Trend Watcher's, is knowing what areas in the vast sea of available information have value and should be exploited. The real "marketing" takes place as soon as the public sees the product. In other words, news sells itself.

What Constitutes News?

News people receive much data about which they are justifiably skeptical. It is often self-serving and therefore carries with it an attempt to influence their decisions about news values. The efforts of public relations "flaks," the huge volume of daily press releases, and people's attempts to stage media events all fall under suspicion as efforts to distort the proper function of the media as a daily mirror. But for all a reporter's good intentions, some information from these sources becomes news. The pressure of competition, the need to report on public figures, the skills of PR professionals in making themselves helpful all have their effects, which show up daily in print and on the air.

News flows don't always fall into neat categories of pure information on one side and media manipulation on the other, as shown in Figure 3-1. The distinction between these two categories blurs when the sources of news all originate with the same point of view.

One of the strengths of the major national news media has been their ability to draw data from a very broad range of sources. Occasionally, one sector or another—the business community, for example, or minority groups—may complain that their view has been omitted. Sometimes, the problem is that the view in question is suspected as being less news and more self-serving hype. For the individual or organization who wants to put forward a point of view, the primary ingredient for success is to show that the public will want to have some of that particular information for its own sake. That is the ultimate market test that editors and reporters employ to ensure that the news filter functions well.

Another aspect of this question is the media-age adage that nothing really happens if the media fail to cover it. This fact of media life is very well recognized by journalists and public relations types. It is expressed differently in different places. Certain newspapers, for example, are recognized as standards of everything that occurs on a given day—"papers of record," in journalism jargon. If an event doesn't make a paper of record, by definition that event goes unrecorded. A corporate disclosure can be a nonevent if it fails to make it in the *Wall Street Journal*. A State Department initiative could die if it isn't recorded in the *New York Times*. Politicos cannot connive without the *Washington Post*.

All of this makes sense. The public doesn't know what it doesn't see, hear, or read. In the modern world, reality has become what the media exposes, much more than the events themselves. Indeed, the information age has engendered what has become known as the media event—an occasion created simply by inducing media coverage. Politicians, pop musicians, and other personalities all share the ability to make things happen simply because they have a near-guaranteed ability to attract public exposure wherever they go and with whatever they do. (Indeed, we call them "media stars.") Increasingly, politicians from the president on down aren't concerned with "How will the public react?" as much as with "How will it be covered?"

Rates of Exposure

As we stated earlier, it is useful to separate the factual events from the volume of media coverage that events receive. Variations in the volume of coverage (or "exposure") determine the degree of significance that the public is led to attach to a given event. News reports confirm that events have occurred. If these events are covered heavily by many news organizations, the events are thought to have occurred in a big way.

If we track the exposure a subject is given in the media, we can begin to see how people are reacting or will react to the news. Fortunately for Trend Watchers, this can be done easily. By averaging the rates of exposure—that is, coverage— given different issues, themes, and events, you can get a fairly clear measure of the information reaching the majority of the public. Ultimately, you can observe the sources of change in society.

The icing on the cake is that you can take care of the news bias problem at the same time. You don't want to know what just one newspaper says; to get an adequate sample of total exposure, you must look at a cross-section of media. By doing so, you can obtain a measure of national exposure, then factor out most editorial prejudice, spin, and other sources of bias. This leaves you with a media-eye view of events. It is something less than Platonic reality, but in today's world it is an accurate view of what the public believes to be happening.

The Collective Mind and the Public Memory

The ultimate recipient of the information process we have just described is the public's collective mind. Occasionally, we get a direct, cause-and-effect glimpse of this action—during elections, for example, or when polls are taken right after a major event. Such occasions give Trend Watchers the chance to see easily how news moves the public to action.

The poor memories of most individuals notwithstanding, the public's collective mind retains a great deal of information. As biologists point out, human memory almost never forgets—subconsciously, at least. This is one of the more astonishing revelations of recent scientific research, and it has bearing on our problem. People store news in their minds, just as they do other data, for later use in the right context. "Stored" news knowledge is brought out as subsequent needs arise to make decisions or form opinions.

Public reaction to news doesn't always occur immediately; it can take considerable time, building slowly. Sometimes, a reaction might not manifest itself for months, even years. And with good reason. It can take time for the public to decide on an appropriate reaction to an event or issue. Should people pass a law, change their habits, pressure their neighbors, or simply write off some disastrous event as a quirk in the system? The reaction process is aided and abetted by the media, which keep feeding the public's mind with the pros and cons of a given issue. People collectively store such data, weigh it in the balance, and determine or set limits to their reactions.

"Public memory" is an important factor in evaluating media exposure. Examples abound in modern history. Perhaps most famous is the consistent West German hypersensitivity to inflation that has lasted since the 1920s. It was reinforced at the end of World War II, and it persists in West German decisions on monetary policy to this day—beyond the lifespan and the individual memories of most people who first encountered the problem. Hypersensitivities have been planted in more recent times, too. Major nuclear accidents like those at Three Mile Island and Chernobyl have riveted not just American, but world public attention. This exposure is retained in the collective public memory of almost everyone in the industrialized world. It is fully predictable that the memory of these accidents will ultimately force public action on a wide range of fronts toward eradicating the threat of poisonous nuclear radiation.

Public memory is fed in two ways. The classic journalism metaphor is rain. *Drip, drip, drip,* even on a piece of granite, and the rock will eventually wear away. In Trend-Watching terms, small amounts of exposure collected in the public memory over long periods of time build up to a force for change. This is a fairly common phenomenon.

A second, and more obvious, method is the mind-shattering punch of huge exposure levels to short-term stories. In the 1980s, these news items have become increasingly common. The impact of blockbuster stories is somewhat different from the slow "drip" method. Often, blockbuster stories are of foreign origin and very frightening. They tend to break up the flow of other news, to divert public attention from more traditional concerns, and to introduce a certain kind of disorganization or uncertainty into the public's mind. In the early 1980s, only one or two stories a year commanded 10 percent or more of all national media coverage in any two-week period. (As stated earlier, ten percent of national coverage is considered the threshhold for a major story, the point at which most people become aware of it.) By 1985, there were 14 such stories. In 1986, there were 23, from the space shuttle and Chernobyl disasters to tax reform and the federal budget deficit.

What is the meaning, in Trend-Watching terms, of such heavy doses of exposure? Consider first the media. It has been forced to regroup constantly, jumping from the Philippines one minute to Nicaragua the next, then on to tax reform, drug abuse, South Africa, the budget, abortion, AIDS, and pornography. Editors say they can handle this constantly shifting load without affecting overall news coverage. But, in fact, national coverage of many long-standing concerns—the environment, for example—has decreased considerably, despite a raft of chemical spills, reports of water contamination, and nuclear waste problems. Still, editors know that these issues remain locked in the public memory; in fact, the public is educated to deal with new issues as they arise, with less explanatory material.

At the same time as editors and reporters are cutting down on "old" issues, they must constantly expand their horizons of interest—their "beats"—to move quickly into new, unfamiliar material as the technological complexity of the world increases. To do this, they must rely once again on public memory; they relate the unfamiliar in terms of ideas and images to which the public has already been exposed. So, however inappropriate to do so, Chernobyl must be explained in terms of Three Mile Island; the Iran-contra affair must be explained in terms of Watergate; and every presidential election must be explained in terms of previous ones.

What about the impact on the public of this increase in major stories? For one thing, people have come to expect blockbusters. A slow news day, it seems, has become one in which only the usual range of events transpires: a few sensational murders, some allegations of corporate or political scandal, some regional weather calamities, an airplane accident, a few million hungry people, a handful of skirmishes on half a dozen international fronts. Regardless of the substance of the stories, the message is that the future will consist of a constant supply of scary stories. Life, at least as seen through the news, will be more frightening, perhaps even somewhat chaotic. The obvious implications are a trend toward demanding better answers on public safety and security. The axis of debate will increasingly cross these issues until people are convinced that their world will be safer and more secure.

The ideas of exposure and public memory can be used to measure trends. Trend Watching will allow you to see where and how the flows of exposure run, to determine what perceptions of events they are delivering, and to predict the consequences. Public memory is crucial to this process because you can see it building, and you know that public reactions can be delayed. Sometime in the future the information in the public memory will be brought to bear as new messages fit with it to produce new insights and, ultimately, new actions.

Public memory, therefore, is a key function of the Trend Watcher's ability to foresee and predict. It is an important aspect of the information flows that allow you to read trends.

Media Sensitivity

Journalists, too, have a function of memory that influences their choice of stories and the volume of news exposure. Selecting news from non-news is an automatic function, part of earliest newsroom training. Journalists become sensitive to certain kinds of stories and tend to ignore others whose credibility cannot be established.

As mentioned earlier in this chapter, the makeup of the news often falls on the judgment—and therefore the prejudices—of a very few people. Some stories get the green light; others never move. Trend Watchers must be particularly aware and be wary of these internal preferences. The preferences may include bias, but are more often the result of decisions about what is news.

We call this phenomenon "media sensitivity," and we can measure it. It is another clue in Trend Watching. By monitoring a flow of events and measuring the amount of exposure per event, you can roughly gauge the degree of importance journalists attach to a story or a subject. Watching media sensitivity is another way of measuring the immediacy of an issue.

Media sensitivity is a measure of the amount of coverage for each story on a given subject. If there are 10 articles about story A that total 500 column-inches, and 20 articles about story B that total 750 column-inches, it can be said that the media are more sensitive to story A, giving it an average of 50 column-inches per story (500 column-inches divided by 10 stories), compared with 37.5 column-inches for story B (750 column-inches divided by 20 stories). Although story B had "more coverage" in the raw number of stories it garnered, story A could be considered more important, having received greater coverage at each appearance.

Let's make something perfectly clear. As Trend Watchers, we are not interested in sitting in judgment on editors and journalists. We are interested only in knowing how the media system works so that we can measure and read the flow of public messages. The media's sensitivity to an issue or a story varies from event to event, from issue to issue. It is a measurable phenomenon that tells us whether an item is hot or cold in the short term, whether there is immediate or long-term concern, and whether interest in an issue is growing or fading.

A Responsible Media

News, as we've said, provokes some kind of action. If the media announce that the chairman of General Motors will hold a press conference, the world speculates. An acquisition? Retirement? A new car model? Public speculation about links between news and action is derived from previous experience. People know the GM top brass will probably not personally announce layoffs or plant closings unless something very important is going on in the corporation. The task of announcing bad news is usually left to press relations staffers, who are paid to make the company look as good as possible under any circumstance.

There are countless ways a piece of news can be taken as the basis for planning future action. We have all learned to look for the next step, just as we jump from the mention of the GM chairman's upcoming press conference to the substance of his announcement. In this way, news serves the public as its root cause of action. It forms a substantial, though not total, part of the data we need to conduct our lives.

Like journalists, people are skeptical about information aimed at getting them to behave in certain ways; after all, no one likes to be manipulated. To some degree, we all perceive when something is just political grandstanding, PR razzle-dazzle, or sales puffery. We are sensitive to ego, emotion, and halos. But we are also influenced by them because, for many people, these manipulative elements are inseparable from the news. News is available as a total package, but we do not all focus on the same elements in it; one person's "news" may be another's useless information. A certain amount of spin, manipulation, and bias will always get through. You can fool some of the people all of the time.

This puts added pressure on the judgments of media managers—newspaper, magazine, and television editors and producers. If their judgments are faulty, the public can make large collective mistakes. If crime reporting is not reflective of reality, for example, people can dangerously relax the security in their homes and businesses or become needlessly paranoid. The only recourse for bad news judgment is in the marketplace: by not buying a publication or not watching a program; or, in a very few cases, by trying to buy out the newspaper, station, or network.

As both Trend Watchers and citizens, we must choose carefully the media we opt to use. The range of choices is often limited to a few available daily media. People who depend on television—increasingly, the dominant force among news media—can choose only among channels; they must pretty much take in an entire program when and how scheduled or ignore it. The advent of the videotape recorders changes this a bit. People can tape a program and view it later, fast-forwarding through the parts they want to skip, but this isn't known to be widely practiced and probably is more trouble than it's worth.

Because some news organizations don't always serve us well, the media themselves become a public issue from time to time. During the 1980s, the major media have demonstrated their growing acceptance of this problem by covering a great deal more news about their own problems. Some organizations have established ombudsmen; others feature media critics. Some of this coverage was driven by events such as libel suits (like one against CBS by former Vietnam General William Westmoreland, for example) and by various mergers and takeovers.

But the media's response to such issues also showed a heightened sensitivity to their own problems. In the first surge of this reporting, much of the coverage was highly self-conscious. Later, media stories settled down to a staple of their agenda, ongoing issues for the 1980s and beyond.

The Power of Negatives

The ongoing tension between the media and the public has turned the news process into a battle over who and what gets exposure during the 30 to 60 minutes of each day's television evening news and in the several thousand column-inches contained in a typical daily paper. Implicit in the fight is a recognition of the value of the prize. Exposure in the media means moving public minds, perhaps eliciting public action. It is worth striving for. Some kinds of exposure, of course, are better than others. Clearly identified, positive stories are generally preferred, but negative stories are more powerful in moving the public's collective mind.

Earlier we described the 1984 Democratic presidential primaries as an example of the public's having to make a choice between two candidates on a series of known dates for successive state-wide elections. In every election, the candidate who won was the person best able to overcome his negatives as reported in the media. Moreover, our weighting system—in which negative stories counted four times more powerfully than all other news—was borne out in the election returns.

This principle is similar to one discovered existing in the consumer marketplace. According to a 1983 study by the Direct Selling Foundation, an unhappy customer will tell nearly a dozen other people about a negative experience; 13 percent of those people will tell 20 others, and on and on. Positive experiences are related only a fraction of the time, however. Negative news brings a similar reaction, having a greater sense of importance, being remembered and talked about by more people for a longer time.

The point is that negative news gets through much more effectively than neutral or positive news. This is what Eric Berne, author of *Games People Play*, called "hooking the unhappy child" in our own personalities. Psychologically, we all tend to retain and worry about negative experiences, comparing them to other information in our minds. Negative news seems to work in a similar way. It gets through, sticks in the memory, and has a strong impact on future action.

On the media battleground of recent years, we have seen a much-increased use of negatives in advertising and political campaigns. Often, the source of the bad news will somehow be detached from the element it is intended to serve. An "unofficial" campaign group will undertake such a role for a candidate, for example, so that the candidate can avoid being tarred with his own brush. (This is the same reason why the president of General Motors usually doesn't announce his company's layoffs or plant closings.) Politicians employ this technique a great deal, relegating bad news to senior officials and unnamed spokespeople. When they must break bad news themselves, it is often done in passive language that removes the speaker from the subject at hand; for example, "Mistakes were made." It is a well-documented peculiarity of negative news that it usually hurts the source as well as the subject. The world has not forgotten the ancient custom of killing the messenger who brings the bad news.

The negative vs. positive news concept is most important with respect to images, as in a political campaign. It also affects attitudes on issues, products, and opinions. Because of the importance of advertising in our society, people tend to see images more in terms of people and products, but ideas and issues have their images, too. Public perception on any given point is usually limited to a very few impressions. One of these is always, "How does this affect me?"

The Value of Distortions

Manipulation, bias, and media sensitivity are boons to Trend Watchers, as are all the other aspects that cause news exposure to be something less than an accurate mirror of public interest and action. If all media reporting were accurate, if it were truly, the "daily mirror," Trend Watching would be too easy and too obvious. The value of watching trends, then, would diminish considerably.

Precisely what Trend Watchers want to see is how events and exposures vary. By noting the shifts in volume, you can determine how interest and attention is being focused and refocused. Often, the difference between the volume of exposure and what previous events have led you to expect is the smoke signal you are seeking. Unexpected discrepancies are the improbabilities you want to spot. You can use them to determine their meaning and recognize trends.

Consider something as mundane as the stock market. Millions of words are written about the state of the economy, and especially about the economic outlook. What few economics reporters seem to know is that gross volume of negative economic coverage, especially when unrelieved by good news, has a direct and depressing effect on everyone. Ignorance extends to newspeople and the public. In this situation, bad news tends to snowball, as newspeople become increasingly sensitive to the possibilities of serious economic problems.

For example, the two sharp stock market downturns in the summer of 1986 were both preceded—by just a few days, but nonetheless preceded—by strong increases in negative news. Before the major 86-point drop on September 11, the volume of negative news during the preceding two-week period had suddenly jumped to more than 5 percent of all national news— a clear signal that the bad news was pushing people to take a highly negative view of the future.

Figure 3-2 illustrates how media coverage of negative economic news affected the stock market during this period of 1986. The point is not just that the media influenced the course of the market, but that everyone involved—including reporters and market insiders—was caught up in the forces created by this heavy flow of negative news, even though virtually no one was aware of this specific signal.

To summarize, media news moves the public's mind, which is the information reservoir from which all social, political, and economic action flows. So if you know how the media

Figure 3-2 The effect of negative economic news in 1986 on the stock market.

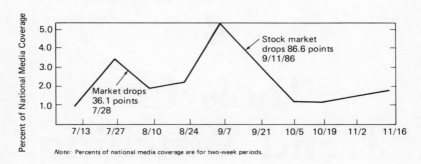

Note: Percents of national media coverage are for two-week periods.

affect the public's mind, you'll have a better idea of where subsequent action is likely to lead. This is the elemental force behind almost all trends in modern society. It is also the force you must measure to become a Trend Watcher.

In the next chapter, we discover the tools with which to measure the news. The first step is examining the mechanics of Trend Watching. Then we can begin to apply these tools to specific problems.

4

Tools for Trend Watching

Fewer than a score of institutions determine the national flow of news in the United States. This condition is lamented variously by media critics as a monopoly, a media dictatorship, a manipulative situation by a media elite, or simply a very poor system of journalism.

None of these descriptions, in fact, is true. National news is, in strict economic terms, something of an oligopoly: dominance by a few. True, the leading journalists come from a relatively elite background; most are male, white, and well educated. But they thrive on disagreement among themselves over what is news and which news items are truly important. And national news is strongly supplemented by media of all kinds at the local level, making monopolies, dictatorships, and manipulations difficult, if not impossible. Moreover, in spite of these limitations, almost any country you can name has fewer major "national" dailies.

The limited number of national news outlets is actually good news for Trend Watchers. It means that, with minimal effort, you can get a good view of the flow of messages regularly sent to the vast majority of Americans. A few media dominate news flows in this country; they are the ones everyone uses in common. They offer a Trend Watcher the few items he or she must measure to read information flows throughout society. By scanning national media, a relatively easy procedure, you can discern a pattern in the news flows that touches all Americans. This gives a common background against which to measure more specific trends.

The Major Media

In the late 1980s, the dominant national media in setting news trends for the United States are:

- three television networks: ABC, CBS, and NBC
- three newsmagazines: *Time, Newsweek* and *U.S. News & World Report*
- five to ten newspapers, of which three must always be included in any national accounting: *New York Times, Wall Street Journal,* and *Washington Post*
- two wire services that act as wholesalers of news: AP and UPI

There are other national papers that demand attention, including the *Christian Science Monitor* and *USA Today,* but they don't dominate what journalists think, as do the *New York Times, Washington Post,* and *Wall Street Journal.* If you travel around America, these three are the out-of-town papers you find on most editors' desks. They also function as the chief written archives for network television news departments. Because television has a difficult time storing and retrieving its own material handily, and because its researchers must find details as background for their broadcasts, these major dailies are the best ready references—hence, their frequent designations by those both in and outside the news business as "newspapers of record."

The *New York Times, Wall Street Journal,* and *Washington Post* have competition from papers beyond the East Coast. Two strong news organizations with dominant flagship papers also have major national influence: the Chicago Tribune Company, which owns the *Chicago Tribune*, among other print and broadcast properties; and the Times-Mirror Company, publisher of the *Los Angeles Times* and owner of a wide range of other media properties, including the influential *National Journal*. Both of these have important syndicate services, a stable of overseas correspondents, and the respect of editors throughout the country. To this list of organizations might be added several others, among them Gannett, which publishes *USA Today*, but which also owns more than 120 other newspapers, mostly in small and midsize cities (like Rochester, New York; Wilmington, Delaware; and Santa Fe, New Mexico); Knight-Ridder Newspapers (Charlotte, North Carolina; Miami, Florida; and San Jose, California); and Hearst Newspapers (Los Angeles and San Francisco, California; and San Antonio, Texas). There are many fine independent papers, too, among them the *Boston Globe, Minneapolis Star and Tribune*, and the *Louisville Courier-Journal*. The extent of their influence differs only by a matter of degree. What a Trend Watcher is looking for at this point are media whose work immediately affects a significant number of other media in building a national news consensus.

Wire services play a special role among the dominant media, but they do not serve a Trend Watcher's needs very well. Monitoring news flows on the wires can be useful, but it gives no clue as to a story's volume of exposure. Wire services, which generate choices for editors but don't directly reveal what editors choose to expose, represent wholesale news that has not yet been put on the market.

Radio also falls from our list of key media, but not because it is unimportant. Almost as many people get their national news from radio as from newsmagazines like *Time* and *Newsweek*. The difference is that, with one or two exceptions, no nationwide radio newscast plays a "dominant" role. Increasingly, the probing work of National Public Radio, with programs like "All Things Considered" and "Morning Edition," reaches this level of influence. But happily for Trend Watchers, radio's time has not yet come again.

Why "happily"? Because monitoring electronic media is much more costly and difficult than monitoring print. If possible, you are better off using only those media that are easy to count. For now, it is fine that radio, whose messages pass fleetingly over the air without creating an easily accessible record, can be bypassed for Trend-Watching purposes.

Other Countries, Other Cultures

Only very big and powerful countries actually have a true "national" media system. European states, by contrast, easily invade each other's turf with electronic broadcasts as well as with print media. Moreover, the multilingual geography of Europe is vulnerable to the combined attractions of that flexible world medium known as "English." This is especially true when it comes to radio and television; the British Broadcasting System's signals extend far beyond the English Channel. It is also true of print media. Many business people in Europe can't do without the *International Herald Tribune,* for example, regarded by some people as the best American newspaper (owned in part by the *Washington Post* and *New York Times*) because it gives an overview of U.S. events and trends with the perspective one gets by taking a few steps away from the subject at hand.

Continental countries like the Soviet Union, China, India, Brazil, and Australia share with the United States an ability to generate a true and almost exclusively national news system. These systems are largely the result of size, invulnerability to other news systems, and years of developing a native news culture.

In the United States, the native news culture is arrogantly strong and nationalistic. Americans take almost all their news, even news from abroad, through domestically controlled channels. The number of Americans who regularly read foreign periodicals or listen to foreign radio broadcasts is very small. Even foreign news services like Reuters and Agence France Presse have relatively few outlets in the United States.

The Media Expand their Market

The demand side for news is what interests Trend Watchers. People want to know the news that affects them. Quite perceptively, they seek news about what is going on in their immediate region or industry and look for meaning in how more distant events will affect them. The growth of local television news at the expense of national news has been notable in the 1980s. From the point of view of Trend Watchers, it is more important, too, than developments in cable or rival network systems, because the increase in local news has changed the pattern of news dominance.

As we have mentioned, news managers—editors, news directors, publishers, and others—must give the public the news it needs and wants. They can expand their markets somewhat by stressing the "wants" rather than the "needs." The latter are all too often unpleasant, whereas the former can be good entertainment. News organizations have a number of options at hand to do this. They can, for example, try one or all of the following:

1. *Rely on identification with personalities.* People prefer to get their news from someone they understand and respect. When "Uncle" Walter Cronkite was credible, so was CBS, and people watched its news broadcasts; when he left, network news supremacy suddenly become a three-way horserace. Cronkite, indeed, helped forge the importance of the news anchor, who has become to news broadcasts what brand names are to breakfast cereals. Demand can be sustained by creating audience links to newscasters.

2. *Exploit controlled sources of supply.* Traditionally, the major television networks and other dominant media have relied heavily on news flowing from Washington, D.C.—"the news capital of the world," according to some. Washington has been the turf of the national media, particularly the networks. That is changing, however, as local stations increasingly produce their own Washington coverage, thanks in part to satellite technology, which allows almost any station to purchase a mobile uplink, enabling it to broadcast live from virtually any

spot on earth. Since many of these transmissions are shared by several stations, Washington politicians and other newsmakers take special care to see that these smaller broadcasters get, if not equal treatment, then reasonable access to their press conferences and other media events.

3. *Use more local news.* The networks, seeing their audiences shrinking, have tried to increase the "local angle" in their newscasts. One technique is to send the anchor to a local city and originate the broadcast from there. Another is to find local stories created by local affiliates and use them nationally. These techniques, however, are only partially effective. Good local newscasts are hard to beat for immediacy, relevance, and credibility. They generate tremendous cash flows, which explains in part why local anchors in major cities commonly are better paid than some network reporters.

4. *Use more foreign news.* Failing to compete on the local level, national media have been looking further afield. Increasingly, national media, with television in the lead, are featuring greater amounts of international coverage. The share of total international coverage doubled between 1982 and 1986, according to our measurements. Much of this has been driven by events and priorities assigned by U.S. foreign policy. The national media have been only too happy to go along. The move to foreign news helped national media in 1985 to hold on to the demand for their services.

Figure 4-1 expresses the peculiar split faced by the national media in meeting their market in the mid-1980s. On one side, demand is highest for news of what is going on close to home. On the other side, the news sources that the major media control most effectively are farthest away, outside the country. It is a poor fit.

But it is not beyond the mind of news managers to establish links between foreign events and local interests. This is what a number of modern sociologists call the "global-local phenomenon." It is the way people in small-town America can empathize with villages in Ethiopia. It is the way the Union Carbide disaster in Bhopal, India, can be linked to risks of chemical leaks in the Kanawha Valley of West Virginia. In

Figure 4-1 National media's supply and demand for news.

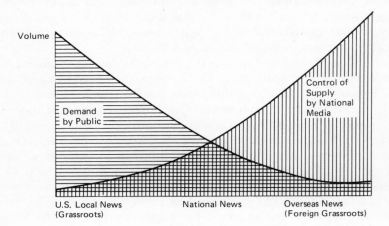

reverse, it is the way demonstrations in front of the South African embassy in Washington, D.C., stimulate opposition to apartheid in Soweto. This expansion of the media's horizon is rapidly changing America's outlook on the world.

For the Trend Watcher, the key point is to note that the global thrust to the news is as much a consequence of the media's needs as that of the events they report. As so often happens in trends, events and reporting are compatible. The boom in foreign news has been very welcome in the boardrooms of CBS, ABC, and NBC; the increase in international coverage in 1985 briefly broke the decline in national news audience.

Pressure to use more news from abroad has had a devastating long-term effect on the news business and on the public's mind. People are beginning to see the world as a whole, not as an appendage of the United States. The boundaries of national news are breaking down. As supply creates demand for better foreign coverage, the demand for news from foreign sources slowly rises.

This is a major phenomenon of our time. As people seek more news from abroad, they begin to call into question the dominance of the national media. Such changes are not yet significant to Trend Watchers, beyond generating some new and interesting data. Someday, however, the monitoring process will have to include material from abroad, just as no measure of trends in Canada today can ignore the fact that about 70 percent of its population is within reach of the U.S. television networks.

Outside Elements Force the Media to Change

Nothing is written in stone, least of all the news and the way the news is written. Today's dominant media can be tomorrow's old-fashioned technologies. Already such titans as the once-dominant newsmagazines and the mighty television networks fight to stay on top of America's changing information-consumption patterns. Editors and producers have explanations for the way news is produced, which often have less to do with news judgments than with market strategies. Those factors may involve problems of supply and demand or the structure of the market itself. Because Trend Watchers are in part media watchers, there are two major factors to keep an eye on.

Takeovers

In the past few years, we have seen how corporate takeovers, or even attempts at takeovers, affect television news style. Ted Turner's attempt to take over CBS in 1986 was accompanied by a softening of CBS's investigative reporting. By moving in a less aggressive manner, the network made itself less vulnerable to the challenge, at the time associated with Turner, that the network carried an anticonservative message. Network officials would strenuously deny any link, of course. Nevertheless, as measured by our National Media Index, CBS increased coverage of conservative issues after Turner—

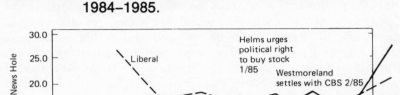

Figure 4-2 CBS coverage of liberal vs. conservative issues, 1984–1985.

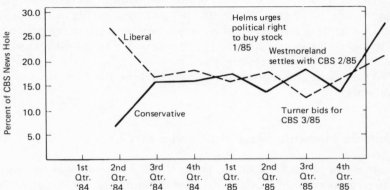

possibly in concert with conservative North Carolina Senator Jesse Helms—mounted a heavy attack in 1985. This kind of softening has been noted by other journalists, if not by CBS's own people. By the same token the shift in NBC's coverage away from 1970s-type liberal issues can be linked almost directly to June 1986, the month General Electric took over the network.

Figure 4-2 shows how CBS's coverage of liberal and conservative issues changed between January 1984 and December 1985. Indicated on the graph are the points at which Jesse Helms urged conservatives to buy CBS stock, the Westmoreland libel suit was settled, and the Ted Turner bid for CBS was made.

For Trend Watchers, the problem is that the cause of these shifts can rarely be pinned precisely on outside influences; editors and producers always claim "news judgment" as the reason for an editorial decision. Still, the reaction to a major challenge to the media's news management is nearly always a move to a preference the public has indicated. CBS became briefly more conservative under pressure from Turner and Helms. It was also reading the 1984 election returns—the ratings, that is. In 1986, when the Democrats retook the Senate and Turner had gone away (even to flirt with the Soviets), CBS once again became the leading network attacking the White House over the Iran-contra affair.

Technology

The effects of changing technology on news judgments are sometimes bizarre. In early 1986, for example, the major media gave far quicker and more effective coverage to an erupting volcano in distant parts of Colombia, South America, than they did to devastating floods in West Virginia, less than 200 miles from Washington, D.C. We recorded 3.8 percent of the volume of news in the period from November 4 through November 17 for the Colombia eruption and 1.5 percent of coverage for the same period for the floods. While it is true that the destruction and number of lives lost was far greater in Colombia, this does not fully explain the media's failure to give full attention to the massive devastation—literally—of entire counties in some of America's finest recreation areas located within a veritable stone's throw of the populated East Coast.

It was easier to get organized for Colombia, it seems, because the drill for getting news from far-off places has become almost routine. Moreover, the Colombia story seemed to have had stronger support from management than the one of reaching out to Appalachia. All this took place, in spite of the fact that the *New York Times*, in a back-page story, later referred to the storm and flood as "the worst in [U.S.] Weather Service history."

It is probably premature to conclude that new technologies such as cable and satellites will radically change the national news system in coming years. A trend toward change, however, is emerging. More news is coming from abroad, for example. Network dominance is under challenge. Increasingly, the national news boundary—the U.S. borders that so few foreign media seem capable of crossing and which are so convenient to major media and Trend Watchers alike—will be penetrated by foreign sources. People may not all be reading *Le Monde* or *Mainichi Shimbun*, of course, but they may soon be seeing BBC broadcasts via satellite, and perhaps even the news, live from Tass.

News, almost by definition, can be sold only where there is a demand for it and where it can be supplied affordably. Technology is costly, untried, and often only marginally threatening to established systems that work fairly well. It was only in the 1970s, for example, that newspapers as a group moved to discard 19th-century linotype systems. News demand, on the other hand, is a much stronger pull. If, at some future time, we *are* all reading *Le Monde* and *Mainichi Shimbun*, it will be because a lot of people wanted to do so in the first place. The media help change demand in response to popular needs and forces in the news market itself. Witness the launching in 1986 of the daily English-language edition of *Pravda*. The success of *USA Today*, aside from its genius of plan and execution, lies in large part in Gannett's correctly identifying the need for a newspaper that would present data quickly and with the splashy color already served up by television. News media seem to use new technology only when popular demand and pressure of competition cannot be dealt with by using present-day systems.

The threat from domestic news sources to the continuing dominance by a few media seems even less likely. One rule we have found useful in watching telecommunications technology is that predicted uses of any new technology are invariably excessive and wide of the mark. For the media oligopoly, the worst won't happen because people will still want to watch and read what others watch and read. Again, readers and audiences herd, just as journalists do.

It is this social herding factor in news production and marketing that makes Trend Watching a worthwhile effort. If people didn't form a consensus at some level on what information they would use to make decisions, they would be unable to reach peaceful and stable agreements as a group. Nor could

Trend Watchers make any sense of information flows. Not only would there be no trends, but there would be chaotic movements in the market and there would also be chaos in making public decisions. Fortunately they do, and we can.

The News Hole

The space or time available to any news organization, print or electronic, to present the news is called the "news hole." Print editors think of it in terms of column-inches, broadcast editors and producers in terms of minutes and seconds. The Trend Watcher looks at the news hole and seeks to recreate editors' decisions, nor just for one paper or television station but for a selected group of media over time. The combined news capacity becomes the Trend Watcher's custom-designed lens through which it is possible to watch changes and trends.

What we have shown so far about the media indicates that there are a handful of news organizations whose influence is so pervasive that they can be taken as a proxy for all national news. You can measure as few as a dozen major media, monitor or measure their news flows, and gain valuable trend information. But to do so requires understanding the process of news production.

We said earlier that what is exposed to the public is the choice, by and large, of editors and their staffs making daily decisions about information flowing in from public sources. Editors control a limited production process. Limits are determined for newspapers and magazines, for example, by the number of column-inches available for each edition. For television news, limits are clearly drawn by the number of minutes in a news broadcast. The print media's news hole varies daily, although it tends toward an average number of column-inches based on such factors as advertising, circulation, and overall financial health of the publisher. For television, the news hole for a half-hour broadcast is about 22 minutes, give or take a few seconds.

Let's leave aside the fact that some of the news hole is measured in time and some in inches; we'll resolve this apples-and-oranges problem later. For now, the important fact is that these media can be observed for a period, during which you can measure each one's average news hole. Taken together, these measurements give a picture of the total capacity of the news system to carry messages to the public. The concept is the same in any system of dominant media, whether in Chicago, Canada, or China. Once you have determined the dominant media, the concept of a total news hole falls into place.

To visualize a national news hole, think of a pie. But instead of showing the pie cut into slices representing news organizations, assign the portions of the pie to various messages the news system is exposing. The pie represents the national news hole; the slices represent the issues the media are covering. Figure 4-3 shows examples of two such national news holes, one by media form (broadcast, newspapers, and magazines) and the other by media category (type of news). As you see, in mid-1986, almost half of the national news hole was filled by the broadcast media; international news took up 37 percent of the news hole. These proportions vary over time.

For Trend Watching, the source of news by a specific news organization—whether the *New York Times* covers Nicaragua with greater intensity than the *Washington Post*, for example—doesn't matter much unless you're doing a media analysis or looking for geographic distribution. To watch trends, you are interested simply in how much of the total news hole is devoted to any one subject at any one time. The goal is to measure usage of that capacity.

Fortunately, you don't need to measure capacity very often. Once you have determined the average number of broadcast-minutes and column-inches in your Trend-Watching sample, you have determined your finite news hole. It becomes interesting to see how that capacity is filled or left void, as the total volume of news rises or falls. Media's use of news capacity at any given time is a helpful gauge of the value editors assign to the current flow of news. There are variations, including

Figure 4-3 National news holes—by media type and category of news.

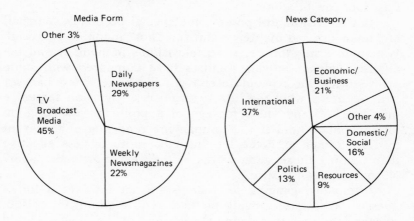

times when news surges (elections, for example) or ebbs (almost every August, and between Christmas and New Year's).

How to Compare Media

One of the Trend Watcher's first problems is determining how to use television and print media. As we said, it's a classic case of apples and oranges: How do four broadcast-minutes of national television coverage compare with 127 column-inches of major print media? Can such a comparison even be made?

The answer is yes. Any news report can be seen as a portion of the space or time devoted to it within its specific medium. In television, 1 percent of total coverage may equal one minute; in newspapers, 1 percent of total coverage may represent 100 column-inches. The figure is different for each news organization. Any given story may be expressed as a percentage of the total time or space available during a given period. Once you reduce the coverage to the common denominator—a share of the total news hole—it is still necessary to determine a formula for linking the effect of, say, one broadcast-minute compared to 100 newspaper column-inches. As you shall see, this, too, can be done.

But television still poses some special problems. Marshall McLuhan stressed that television is a "hot" medium. In Trend-Watching terms, this refers to television's immediacy and the different impact moving pictures have compared with static print stories. Most people aren't visually literate; few can say with accuracy what the full message of a television sequence may be. Will the video footage of a politician speaking on foreign policy (and the accompanying reporting of the event by Dan Rather or Peter Jennings) be more or less effective than reading those same words in the next morning's paper? No one knows for sure.

Ultimately, gauging television's impact involves a lot of guesswork because moving pictures send a whole set of sub-surface messages that define the context of the news and add emotion and color. In television news, the audience invariably picks up background messages from reporters and anchors. Not all such messages are neutral; some can be made very strong, whether it be through voice inflection, raised eyebrows, choice of words, or juxtaposition of words and pictures. The impact has much to do with immediacy. News seems to have the strongest impact when it is happening, so television has a much greater ability than print to deliver that immediacy.

But pictures also deliver ambivalent messages. Yasir Arafat's unshaven face may make him popular in Cairo, but it certainly hasn't helped his image in Europe or the United States. Emotions are conveyed by pictures in the same way they are conveyed in face-to-face conversation. In other words, there is nonverbal communication that only television can offer. At times, these nonverbal communications must be catalogued very carefully, especially when studying the impact of personalities on an audience. For now, however, we won't pay much heed to these subtleties.

One case in which the "hot" factor of television clearly has special impact is during a major story that the public is following carefully and for which the volume of coverage is very high. In these instances, the behavior of reporters and sources becomes itself an artifact of the news flow. Thus, in the 1986 Chernobyl nuclear disaster, the behavior of reporters upon receipt of early, sometimes highly exaggerated data was a key part of the messages sent to the American public. The stronger the message, the greater the role of the messenger. In times of trouble, people tend to hang on television's every word and picture.

Newspapers Are the Daily Record

Regardless of television's instant impact, it is much too early to write an epitaph for the print media. The newspaper is a daily archive for many Americans. It permits them to select the news they want to read or, for some, to keep a file on for ready reference. Even television researchers use clips from print media, often "borrowing" the same experts and sources. Newspapers present details in ways television can't (or, at least, chooses not to). In many ways, this is a compensation for television's emotional impact.

The focus of all but a few newspapers in America is on a specific metropolitan area. Even the *New York Times* and *Washington Post* double as both national and local papers. Newpapers gain immediacy by being physically close to their beats, in a sense competing with television's ability to offer live, on-the-scene coverage.

Newspaper coverage, because it is more detailed, offers a broader opportunity for monitoring special aspects or subsets of data linked to a specific trend. The mix is richer. The *New York Times*, for example, does much more on science, the arts, and foreign affairs; the *Washington Post* is heavy on politics; the *Chicago Tribune* is strong on agriculture and commodities. Trend Watchers are thereby offered a chance to move closer to their particular interests through a specific source. This is the flip side of the print media's "cafeteria" style of supplying news. People can choose what they want, and they are offered different things to attract them; some people carefully read foreign affairs coverage, while others head directly to the sports section. Most people do not read all of a newspaper, while most do watch an entire television news program.

Given these factors, the impact of newspapers is more indirect than that of television. A reader may catch only a headline or read only part of a story. Nevertheless, a consistent reader of the paper will be prepared to "pick up on" a story if its development eventually becomes of interest. The continuity of contact with readers is a key function of communicating via newspapers. Small bits of a story pass to readers over time, and their cumulative effect is often very strong. In this way, relatively small amounts of coverage can have major effects on public behavior.

Television news tends to concentrate on a few big stories, usually only 10 to 12 in a half-hour newscast. Newspapers carry 40 to 50 stories in a single issue, sometimes more. The depth of a newspaper's probe is often greater, and, therefore, provokes deeper reader interest. The effects on subsequent public behavior are correspondingly different. Television will more likely move people immediately, or it will leave a deep, lasting memory of a tragedy, as it did in 1984 with a few minutes' footage of hungry children in Ethiopia—an effect which managed to accomplish what years of print stories hadn't been able to do, by inspiring such international relief efforts as Live Aid. Newspapers, for their part, carry articles on a broad range of public issues, provoke trends in thinking, and keep subjects alive long after the television pictures fade.

Newsmagazines Are the Happy Medium

Newsmagazines offer many options similar to newspapers. The major national publications—*Time, Newsweek,* and *U.S. News & World Report*—tend to blend the "hot" impact of color photojournalism found on television with the "cool," more in-depth coverage of newspapers. Their strength is in their ability to deliver a concise compendium of news to a mass audience, thus relieving readers of having to digest more massive print sources. Until television overtook them, newsmagazines had been a dominant, influential form of national news. Still, for many groups, especially upper-middle-income families, newsmagazines are a basic source of information and they have a strong effect on public thought.

To Trend Watchers, the particular advantage of magazines is precisely that they offer a quick review of subject matter over a short period, minimizing the amount of monitoring required. While newspapers take some time to count, magazines provide more accessible summaries. This feature offers Trend Watchers several options to broaden the scope of surveillance. By selecting relatively few magazines, you can cover a wide area of general or specific interest and take advantage of their concise and compact method of delivery.

Specialized Media Offer Views of the Future

To get ahead of public reaction, Trend Watchers often must look into "precursor" publications. We have so far focused on the national news mix because that is where most people get some news, and it is a common system you cannot do without. But neither national, local, nor regional media regularly deal in specialized information. Nor do they generally carry the forecasts of influentials or leaders—scientists, for example, or social theorists—whose thinking and efforts can start the chain of information that ultimately leads to and moves the public. With few exceptions, the esteemed columnists who appear on opinion-editorial pages are journalists; while their views may be on the leading edge of some issues, these writers are more often than not serving as reporters of other experts' views.

Indeed, one strongly held school of Trend-Watching thought is that forecasts of influentials are all you need to track these trends. In some respects, we dissent from that view. Information does not move people to action until it has been fed into a national system of dissemination. Moreover, the process of public messaging and behavior generates factors of its own, like the actions the media take in response to the demand for news, which strongly influence public behavior. But when it comes to very specialized problems that the general media do not touch, or when long lead times are required to plan or predict trends, precursor media are essential.

Some precursor magazines—the *New England Journal of Medicine* and *Science*, among others—are already recognized by reporters for their influence. When they can, reporters use the views of influentials and results of research as the basis for their stories. They, too, want to be precursors of change. But there are no doubt other periodicals fitting the specific needs of certain Trend Watchers that haven't yet been "discovered."

In evaluating a precursor journal, it is important to know who the audience is, what "downstream" publications are influenced by its output, and how the journal is regarded in its field. A magazine that isn't read by people who can act on its information is hardly an effective precursor of change. On the other hand, a magazine that is too close to the media won't be very far ahead of events. An ideal precursor is one that has gained high marks from its peer group and is just beginning to grow and be discovered.

Magazines that we have found particularly useful for general issues work are *Demography*, *Science News*, and *Utne Reader*, a digest of items from the liberal alternative press. On the other hand, *Business Week* and the *Wall Street Journal* do not make suitable precursors, even though they do a lot of good, in-depth reporting. The problem is that their readership is so large and already so influential that by the time something appears in either of these publications it is no longer at the forefront of a trend; it is already fact.

The value of the precursor to the Trend Watcher is in spotting changes in the flow of information at the earliest possible stage. It is at this point that improbabilities, or changes, can be noted; as they move down the stream of information to the public, they generate trends. Seen in context with other trend movements, signals from precursors can be especially valuable in forecasting or in determining the dynamics of change in any given set of issues.

Precursors are most valuable when viewed in tandem with trends in the general media. In this way the meaning of their messages falls into context, not only with other data about their own particular sectors, but also with broader trends in society as a whole. A Trend Watcher must always maintain a sense of the universe of news, even while watching particular interests. This question of context, which can be solved by looking at trends from both particular and general views, is crucial to effective trend analysis. It requires an ability to move from the particular to the general in rapid order. Indeed, one of the major advantages of Trend Watching is the capacity to do just this.

The Local Angle

Most Trend Watchers, like most people, want to know most about what is happening close to them. Usually, they also want to know something about movements in different geographic regions of the country. Fortunately, we have a lode of local newspapers and television newscasts to mine for this purpose, as well as a growing number of local and regional magazines.

Trend Watchers have several possible uses for local media, although the purposes and techniques of these uses are not all the same. Scanning a broad cross-section of newspapers—say, from state capitals—provides extremely useful trend data derived from the movement of events. Key signals—the improbabilities suggesting change—can be found. As similar events occur in different places, you can infer that somehow communication among key actors is taking place and that a trend is underway.

A few specific instances at the local level are often enough to indicate a major break with the past. For example, if you were involved in the phone business, you would have wanted to know fairly early about the public's feeling concerning changes in local telephone service and rates in the mid-1980s. If you had monitored no more than half a dozen mid- to big-city papers, it is likely you would have spotted some very definite trends on consumer attitudes toward both local phone companies and the plethora of competing long-distance carriers. Such information would have been extremely helpful to a firm marketing any kind of telephone-related product or service directly to consumers.

Megatrends author John Naisbitt demonstrated the high value of using local papers to spot events as precursors of change. In his method, local papers are used just as national media might be. Counting the appearance of stories in local papers, which Naisbitt termed "events," he was able to spot movements that he could then trace as trends over the entire nation. Using local newspapers as national precursors, however, is extremely labor- and time-intensive. It requires counting a wide swatch of papers and summing up their contents.

But local media do have a great and immediate value in terms of communicating within their own areas. They allow Trend Watchers to treat the communities, states, or regions as microcosms of a larger universe. In doing so, a Trend Watcher can produce data using local media exposure that is fully comparable to a larger situation, and gain valuable additional insight about leads and lags among a local area, a marketplace, and the nation as a whole.

Using Local Television

The striking fact about local media is the growing power of local television news. Its importance is increasing in comparison to both the networks and the local papers. The difference in range of content between local television and local newspapers is also much narrower. Not only are there often fewer newspapers, but news holes in local papers are smaller. On the other hand, many local television newscasts are longer than network broadcasts. The total amount of electronic news exposure in most U.S. cities today may be greater than that of print media. This is quite the reverse of national patterns.

Local television newscasts deal much more with individual needs. Once you factor out sports, weather, and possibly crime stories, there are nuggets to be found in excellent local reporting on consumer affairs, health, the environment, and many other social issues.

The Multilens Approach

America is so big, so broad, and so varied that it is perhaps arrogant to suggest that all people are going to conform to any given set of ideas. They don't, of course. There are more views on any given issue than you can possibly count. But this does not prevent you from finding patterns in these ideas. You can see in a general way where public thinking is headed and what public action is likely to be, especially when the choices of action are fairly narrow, as in an election.

The surprising aspect of America is that there is as much conformity as there is. For Trend Watchers, merely watching the big movements probably isn't enough. You will want to know how change will directly affect people. Some of the broad national movements, such as a call for increased corporate responsibility and philanthropy, will not. But many others will provide clues to what additional information is needed and will have a direct, significant effect, whether close to home or within a broad area of interest.

People receive messages from a wide variety of sources. They all share national news in common. They also look at local and specialized publications that circulate in the hundreds of thousands, if not in the millions. In fact, people take in information at several levels. So, too, should an effective Trend-Watching system. Trend Watchers need to gain a perspective, to have a variety of dimensions to their views of change. This can be done best by looking at the news flow on two levels. The first level is always the national media, because it is the set of messages that all people in the country hold in common. If, for example, you are concerned about changing views on nuclear power in your region or community, you can be certain that a great deal of the information local people have received on this subject has come from the national media. Nuclear power is a good example of an issue that has a constantly growing horizon. It is now, since Chernobyl, even an international concern.

The second level to watch can be defined by either geography or business sector. You may be most interested in action in your own state or region. If you are a Westerner operating at some distance from East Coast news centers, a state-level scan of, say, California or Texas could be very useful. On the other hand, if you are in an industry facing change in the market place and possibly are threatened with image problems, a business-based scan of your industry or profession might be more helpful. Of course, there is no reason you can't have both, if you are prepared for the cost and time involved.

Later on, in Chapter 6, we shall look into the task of analyzing trends from two different perspectives. The difficulties are easily overcome; analysis is not the main problem. Trend Watchers use essentially the same analytical methods at whatever level they are looking at. The main advantage of using two perspectives is the extra dimension it gives you to spot leads and lags between the two systems and to see how broader trends are affecting the home turf.

A Final Word About News

We have discussed the operations of the news system in the United States because it is from news flows that the Trend Watcher will find the most useful information. We have argued that there is a significant difference between the pace of events causing the news and the amount of attention the media pays to those events; this difference offers an opportunity to yield additional trend information. We have also suggested that the public retains in its collective memory the news exposures it has received in the past. Over time these memories will fade, if for no other reason than because of passing generations. But in the near term, they remain very firmly part of the public scene, ready to resurface when there is provocation. These memories become one of the key factors in foreseeing future reaction to problems. If you know public memory is strong and negative on an issue, you have solid grounds for predicting future reactions. Trend Watching helps to codify and measure this force. Public memory is one of the tools you have to predict trends.

What we haven't said and won't say is that any specific small group of people receiving information from the media is necessarily going to act in a certain way. We are talking about broad aggregates of messages as they affect a broad public. We don't argue, for example, as some have, that members of Congress are directly cued by the media. They are not necessarily told what to think, even though they are acutely aware of public exposure.

The response of congressional representatives to the media is, however, a good example of how media exposure works. These men and women are well aware of messages going to the public at both national and local levels. Most of them have determined some way of reading changes in the public's mind, and use the media for this purpose. In other words, they are not looking at the media as a guide to what to think; they look at the media as the daily mirror of what voters are being led to think. They often ask themselves how their positions on an issue give them the right exposure, reacting precisely to the role of the media as a mover of the mass mind. This is Trend Watching at its ultimate.

While news moves the public mind and is the information agent that causes most social change in America today, it is unclear whether it also affects individual behavior. Individual readers or viewers are selective in what they see and retain. It is incorrect to assume, as some advertisers did in the 1950s, that scattershot ads could move individuals to buy certain products. It is a bit more complicated than that. An item of news is part of the broader force of all news and information. Trends develop from the interaction of massive flows of news and mass behavior of people. To be more precise is to carry the analogy much too far.

So far, we have shown how media play a role in Trend Watching; and we have begun to show how you can select individual media to provide a proper data base. The data base is the specially designed news hole through which you can gain a new perspective on the world. Now you are ready to begin Trend Watching.

5

Determining What You Want to Know

Whether you are tracking a few issues or a hundred, you'll use the same four basic Trend-Watching steps. We'll cover these steps in this and the next three chapters.

Chapter Five: Determining What You Want to Know
Chapter Six: What Media to Count
Chapter Seven: Counting and Calculating
Chapter Eight: Analyzing and Predicting

What Do You Want to Know?

The first step of the Trend-Watching process is simply to list the things you want to know. Because one key to success in Trend Watching is determining cause-and-effect relationships among various seemingly unrelated matters, inevitably you will be tracking several issues at once, perhaps a dozen or more. Try to capsulize these issues with titles—simple terms that will help you watch the movement of your topics over a period of time. If you are interested in housing, for example, your capsulized titles might include Construction Costs, Finance, Zoning, and Housing Styles. Make the list as broad as possible, and include everything you think is important. Then pare it down to a manageable list of no more than 50 items, including both major headings and subcategories.

Determining the answer to "What do you want to know?" usually isn't as simple as it may seem at first blush. Let's assume for the moment that you own a small chain of retail stores in the Pacific Northwest selling gardening products. Your product line includes lawn mowers and other gardening tools, seeds, fertilizers, soils, bulbs, flowers, plants, planters, garden furnishings, and assorted decorative items. The principal question confronting you will be broad and sweeping—something like, "What are the prospects for my company over the next few years?"

To answer that question, you must first look at several factors. You will need, for example, to carefully define your informational universe. Trying to track every issue related to gardening products could be unwieldy. On the other hand, if you don't track some related—and some seemingly unrelated— gardening issues, you will be viewing your area of interest without the full perspective necessary to answer your question of principal concern.

It's important to understand that you won't be counting and calculating every article in every publication you read or scan. You will be looking for selected subjects of interest, however narrow or broad those subjects may be. As we've stated earlier, you probably are already reading the right publications and noting the stories of interest. In Trend Watching, your unconscious or intuitive tracking process will be given some discipline, enabling you to quantify and analyze that tracking.

The idea, then, is to begin with the broadest view possible of your gardening product universe, then to prune that broad view to obtain a manageable universe of subjects. You want that universe to yield the broadest possible perspective of the world important to your gardening business.

It is easiest to go from the general to the specific in simple steps. Begin by breaking out the major issues or themes you think are important. For example:

- The economy
- Housing issues
- Manufacturers' and products' images
- Environmental issues
- Health issues

Ultimately, this list may give you eight to ten major categories. The next step is to break these major categories into subsets. For example:

- State of the Economy
  Employment
  Prices
  Local growth and development
- Housing (other than construction)
  Landscaping
  Architecture
  Preferences
- Gardening Products
  Fertilizers
  Plants
  Other
- Product Issues
  Safety
- General Environment
  Air pollution
  Water pollution
  Land preservation
  Animal protection
  Weather

- Health
  Diseases
  Physical fitness
  Nutrition
  Costs

Having gone this far, you can see that some of your subsets may need even further breakdown. For example, "Product Safety" could refer to the health aspects of generic gardening products such as pesticides, which themselves could be broken down further into specific products and types of chemicals. Similarly, "Physical fitness" could be subdivided to show pluses and minuses of gardening activity: exercise, for example, on the positive side; muscle strain on the negative. Note that as you move deeper into subordinate issues, the subject matter becomes closer to the immediate concerns of the business. Using positives and negatives is, of course, very important with images; each of the corporate names and brands you track for image exposure should have positive and negative subsets.

It is important to move from the general to the specific and to allow for both perspectives. A key element of Trend Watching is learning how general movements reach down and affect specific individuals and vice versa. You can add as many subsets for a given issue as you like.

The hard part in this process is often the one that seems easiest: making a good set of general issues in the first step. You don't want to leave out any broad aspect that could be important. To be comprehensive you may want to set up a broad category like "Social Values" that would allow you to deal with such contingencies as rising concern over neighborhood crime, and how that concern might lead to fences and other security measures, which could affect the landscaping business.

Another important reason for moving from the general to the specific is to allow you to set up categories that are as mutually exclusive as possible. In this way your counts will fit easily and naturally into assigned categories, and you won't have to fret over where an article on a certain subject should be placed. For your system to be accurate, don't place the same bit of news reporting in two different categories. Double-counting will distort your perspective by giving too much weight to items you haven't defined correctly (more on this in Chapter Seven).

Editors will help you. Most news coverage, especially in newspapers, tends to be organized into articles on clearly defined subjects. That's what editors aim for, and you should let them do your work for you. When it comes to counting column-inches and broadcast-minutes, there should be very few articles that must be divvied up among different categories. If you have difficulty deciding whether, say, an item about a pesticide falls under "Product safety" or "Air pollution," you can solve the problem at the outset by noting cross-references among items on your issues list. For example, a problem with releasing chemical gasses into the air might fall in either category. Your data entry should note that. This helps with later analysis, and will tide you (or whoever is doing the counting) over until a list of clear definitions has been established.

Once you get going, you may find that your issues list reflects your trade or your industry's perspective exclusively. That's not good. It must also reflect what your customers are hearing and thinking about issues that could influence their purchases. To compile that list, start with the obvious issues that affect supply and demand for gardening products in the community. Those factors can be added as subsets, or sub-subsets, to the list given earlier. For example:

The local economy. Your products aren't essentials, so they will be among the first things people give up when times get tough. Clearly, local employment trends will be one barometer of future sales. To adequately follow employment trends in your Pacific Northwest region, you'll want to track the major employers and industries—Boeing Corporation, for example, and the paper and lumber industries.

Home construction. An upturn in local home construction will be good news for two reasons: It signals a robust local economy as well as a boom time for the local lumber industry. That prosperity should be reflected in sales at your stores.

Home prices are another factor. High home prices could depress the sale of new and existing homes, leading home buyers to delay purchases. Present homeowners might decide to hold on to their current homes, perhaps adding on or fixing them up, including tackling that long-neglected backyard gardening project.

Energy prices. This factor could have a dual and conflicting impact. On one hand, most fertilizers are petroleum derivatives; changes in price and availability of crude oil will have a definite effect on fertilizer prices. On the other hand, a sharp rise in oil prices could cause a reduction in vacation travel, meaning that people will stick closer to home and probably pay more attention to their gardens.

Food prices. The hard times accompanying the inflation and recession of the mid-1970s revitalized people's interest in growing at least some of their own food—even in big cities, where community gardening plots became (and still are) popular. This already established cause-and-effect relationship is worth watching closely.

Your list of potential issues is growing, but is not yet complete. The last part of your list is the most difficult to compile because it requires answering an intuitive question: "What are the *non*obvious issues that could affect demand for your products?" The answers could be anything from the ridiculous to the sublime. Two possibilities:

1. *Education.* Attitudes toward reading, especially about gardening, are a clue to links between buying books and later purchases of other items.

2. *Sports.* There is a possible trade-off between gardening and other uses of leisure time.

The list could go on, with good reason. Nearly everything, it seems, is interrelated. The challenge is to sort out those issues that are truly important and that have relevance to your business. To jog your memory and round out your issues list, check the National Media Index, included in this book's Appendix, as a helpful resource to key subjects.

Using Other Sources

There's a bit of *Catch-22* operating here. In order to compile a comprehensive issues list, you may need to choose at least some of the media you will be tracking to monitor these issues. The media you track will, to a large extent, dictate which issues you should be watching. In other words, you will be using media to help identify an issues list, which you will use to determine which media to track.

To ferret out the relevant issues for your gardening products stores, you might turn, for example, to *Garden Supply Retailer*, a magazine that covers the gardening industry, and *Hardware Age*, which covers hardware stores, including those that carry many types of gardening "hardware." By looking back through a few months' issues of such publications, you will begin to accumulate a list of subjects.

You will want to follow trends in other areas, too. If, for example, you believe the Pacific Northwest "imports" market trends from California or New England, you will want to consult such publications as *Sunset* or *Yankee*, or even have a look at *Southern Living* for balance.

It is wise to make your list with broad headings and subheadings. The broad view you take should include both the objective—factual things, such as the economic growth rate and home-building rates—and the subjective—such as public tastes and attitudes. But it is important not to have topics overlap. It is difficult, but you must be dogmatic in deciding whether an article is stronger as an event, an image, an issue, or a theme. The choices you make in assigning topic names to these articles—as any librarian can tell you—will determine the ultimate quality of your product. It is therefore essential that you be absolutely clear in your own mind about the definitions.

Things can get confusing at times. Suppose, as a gardening supply store owner, you come across an article about how fertilizers containing organic chemicals have been seeping from topsoil into ground water, which has made its way into the local water supply, which as a result is becoming increasingly polluted. The story further says that the ground pressures forcing the fertilizers into the water supply may be associated with the recent heavy rainfall.

How do you categorize such a story? Under "Weather"? "Water pollution"? "Gardening products"? The answer depends on the way you make your list up based on your own priorities. A traditional list of broad issues would probably call this news item a "Water pollution" issue, using "Fertilizers" as a subset, with a cross-reference to the product or chemical involved. As a gardening supply store operator, however, you are always going to be in the fertilizer business; it is one of your major product lines. Therefore, you should make fertilizers your focus, cataloging the story in terms of the product. In other words, your issues list for this subject would look something like this:

A. Gardening Products
   1. Fertilizers
      a. Organic chemicals
         i. Impact on environment
      b. Inorganic chemicals
         i. Impact on environment

You may wish to cross-reference this story with "Weather" on your weekly count sheet. You can do this easily by putting an asterisk or footnote in the column containing the "Gardening Products—Fertilizers—Organic chemicals—Impact on environment" category, then mentioning below that this story also had to do with local weather.

After you've listed as many issues as you can, organize your items into logical categories, keeping in mind both the broad perspective and your own needs. Our gardening supply store list, for example, might look something like this:

Sample Issues List for Gardening Supply Store Operator in Pacific Northwest

A. State of the Economy
   1. Employment
      a. National
      b. Regional (subset by industry)
      c. Local (subset by major employer)
   2. Prices
      a. Energy
      b. Food
      c. General
      d. Product
   3. Local growth and development
      a. Construction
         i. Homes
         ii. Other
      b. Real estate activity
      c. Small businesses
      d. Park development
      e. Investment (subset by item)
B. Housing (other than construction)
   1. Landscaping (subset by style or design)
   2. Architecture (subset by style)
   3. Preferences
C. Gardening Products
   1. Fertilizers (subset by general category)
   2. Tools (subset by general category)
   3. Machinery (subset by general category)
   4. Seeds (subset by general category)
   5. Plants (subset by general category)
   6. Other (subset by general category)
D. Product Issues
   1. Safety (by brand name)
   2. Manufacturer (by company)
   3. Recommendations (by brand name)
   4. Criticism (by brand name)

E. General Environment
   1. Air pollution
   2. Water pollution
   3. Land preservation
   4. Animal protection
   5. Weather
F. Health
   1. Diseases
   2. Physical fitness
   3. Nutrition
   4. Costs
G. Leisure Time and Recreation
   1. Outdoor recreation
   2. Spectator sports
   3. Gardening clubs
   4. Activities of key groups
      a. Elderly
      b. Handicapped
      c. Singles
      d. Ethnic groups
H. Education
   1. Environmental
   2. Scientific
   3. General
I. Public Policy
   1. Taxes
   2. Zoning (cross-reference to Real estate activity)
   3. Regulation (cross-reference to Product Issues—Safety)
   4. Government spending

   This list may not be complete, nor does it need to be; it's simply a starting point. The key challenge is to analyze your gardening supply business—including its products and the environment in which you do business—into logical categories that correspond to the types of stories you see in the media.
   This first step, like all aspects of Trend Watching, may be a bit difficult the first few times, but practice makes perfect.

You will find, as your Trend-Watching skills develop, that you are more readily able to recognize the links between many seemingly disparate elements of your business. Indeed, if you achieve nothing else in the Trend-Watching process, you will gain considerable insight into your business from this step alone, examining perhaps for the first time how what you do affects, and is affected by, the world around you.

Following are three sample issues lists for three very different needs. They show how lists may vary from one set of interests to another. Still, you will see that many of the basic categories remain the same, even though they serve different users with different interests. It is worth underscoring that no tailor-made issues list is going to save you from having to design your own. The choices made and the methods of presentation used determine the scope—and very often the success or failure—of your Trend-Watching effort.

Issues List 1: Campaign for County Commissioner

The time is long gone when local politicians can count on election victory with a few stump speeches. Today's local leader has got to know a great deal about many issues. The list is necessarily long and complex. It also has a business side; the candidate's list must have several dimensions, ranging from voter issues to campaign problems to how local government is working—or isn't.

A. Key Voter Issues
    1. National (subset by broad categories)
    2. State (by broad categories)
    3. County
        a. Consumer issues (subset cross-reference)
            i. Air service
                (a) Traffic delays
                (b) Safety
        b. Crime
            i. Courts and criminal justice

        ii. Prisons and parole
      iii. Police
      iv. Specific problems
  c. Education
        i. High schools
          (a) Policy
          (b) Specific school
       ii. Elementary schools
          (a) Policy
          (b) Specific schools
      iii. Pre-school
  d. Environment
        i. Toxic waste (by case)
       ii. Air pollution (by case)
      iii. Water pollution (by case)
          (a) Surface water
          (b) Ground water and drinking water
      iv. Conservation
          (a) Land (by case)
          (b) Wildlife (by case)
  e. Health
        i. Diseases (by item)
       ii. Care (by delivery system)
      iii. Costs
  f. Infrastructure
        i. Buildings
       ii. Roads, highways and bridges
      iii. Sewage disposal
      iv. Emergency services
       v. Utilities
  g. Social Issues
        i. Child care
       ii. The aged
      iii. Equal rights
          (a) Ethnic groups
          (b) Women
      iv. Immigration, etc.

B. The Campaign
    1. Candidates' images
        a. Self
            i. Positive
           ii. Negative
        b. Opponents (by individual)
            i. Positive
           ii. Negative
    2. Techniques (cross-reference to Candidates)
    3. Funding issues (by candidate)
    4. Political parties
    5. Contributors (by source)
C. The Economy
    1. Positive items
        a. New payrolls
        b. Investments and development
    2. Negative items
        a. Layoffs
        b. Bankruptcy
    3. Money issues
        a. Interest rates
        b. Credit
        c. Institutions (banks, etc.)
        d. Labor relations (by case)
D. Fiscal Issues
    1. Budgets (by spending increases and cuts)
        a. Federal
        b. State
        c. Local
    2. Taxes
        a. Federal
        b. State
        c. Local
E. Media
    1. Television (by station)
        a. Ownership
        b. Programming
    2. Print media (by publication)

      a. Ownership
      b. Programming
F. Social Behavior
    1. Recreation and leisure activities (by subject)
    2. Entertainment and culture
    3. Dress
    4. Consumption patterns
    5. Sports
G. Morality and Ethics
    1. Religion (by denomination or institution)
    2. Issues
      a. Bio-ethics
      b. Animal welfare

Issues List 2: Corporate Personnel Manager

The corporate official can be more specific than the political candidate, looking for details of recruitment, training, corporate culture, and related matters. The official also, however, needs a general setting. In this case it is the economy that must be watched to spot changes in the demand and supply for skills. Selecting subject matter in this example becomes a good deal more subtle, as the personnel manager seeks to know what is going on in the minds of corporate staffers and those who might replace them. Moreover, there is a need to know a good bit about social behavior and social trends, an even more subjective business than politics. The trends produced, however, can help reduce the guesswork and provide a firmer foundation for projections. They also put a company well ahead of its competition.

A. The Economy (General)
    1. Negatives
      a. Layoffs
      b. Bankruptcy
    2. Positives

       a. New investment
       b. Growth areas
B. Technical Change
    1. Innovation
       a. Processes
       b. Products
    2. Research and development (by case)
C. Education and Training
    1. Source institutions
       a. University level
              i. Personnel
             ii. Program
            iii. Administrative issues
       b. Secondary
              i. Personnel
             ii. Program
            iii. Administrative issues
    2. On-the-job training
       a. Programs (by job category)
       b. Innovations (cross-reference to Technical Change)
D. Health
    1. Costs
       a. Insurance
       b. Medicare
    2. Benefits
       a. Insurance
       b. Medicare
    3. Disease (by item)
    4. Quality of care
E. Welfare
    1. State and federal programs
       a. Benefits
    2. Corporate policy and practice
       a. Home company
       b. Others
F. Demography
    1. Age
    2. Sex

    3. Income level
    4. Migration
    5. Immigration
G. Personnel Behavior
    1. Use of leisure time
    2. Consumption patterns
    3. Clothing habits
    4. Sexual behavior
    5. Associations and memberships
H. On-the-Job Issues
    1. Security
        a. Crime (by type)
        b. Physical safety
    2. Commutation
    3. Travel on duty
    4. Use of free time
I. Industrial Relations
    1. Unions
        a. Contracts
        b. Strikes
    2. Employee ownership
    3. Management systems
    4. Employee rights

Issues List 3: Private Investor

Trend Watching is not in itself a sure way to make a killing in the market. But if you know something about where things are going, you may well get ahead of the herd. Trends may, paradoxically, tell you what not to do. If you're a "contrarian"—one who goes against the crowd—the trend may tell you just where the crowd is going and where you should go to get away from it. In either case, the data can be used effectively.

    The investor's list that follows focuses on the sectors and companies in which such a person would be interested. It may, therefore, be fairly short and suitable for "minimalist" treatment, as we'll explain further in Chapter Six. Again, the investor first must have a fix on trends in the general market. Then he can use trend data on corporate performance effectively.

A. General Economy
    1. Positives
        a. Growth sectors
        b. Good news
    2. Negatives
        a. Declining sectors
        b. Bad news
B. Government Policies
    1. Budgets
        a. Cuts (by area)
        b. Spending (by area)
    2. Taxes
        a. Personal deductions
        b. Corporate incentives
C. Money and Credit
    1. Credit
        a. Interest rates
        b. Supply
    2. The dollar
    3. Institutions
        a. Performance
        b. Regulation
    4. Price changes
    5. Financial markets (by type)
D. Innovation (subset by target sectors)
    1. Communications (by company)
    2. Health (by company)
    3. Energy (by company)
    4. Transport, etc.
E. Positive Performance (as above by sector and company)
F. Negative Performance (as above by sector and company)
G. Labor Relations
    1. Strikes, work stoppages
    2. Contracts

   3. Labor supply
   4. Employee ownership
H. Regulation (cross-reference to Money and Credit)
   1. Consumer protection (by product)
   2. Environment (by affected sector)
   3. Public safety (by sector; for example, nuclear power)
   4. Rates (by sector)
   5. Antitrust
I. Corporate Governance
   1. Management skills (by company)
   2. Personnel (by company)
   3. Scandals/allegations
J. Marketing
   1. Trade advantages (including international)
   2. Advertising (by product)
   3. Market share, etc.
   4. Sales (by company, cross-reference to Positive or Negative Performance)

You get the idea. The issues list, as we've stated earlier, is the backbone of any Trend-Watching system. You are well advised to concentrate your efforts here before proceeding. Once you are comfortable with your list, it is time to tackle the next step—picking the right media.

6

What Media
to Count

Measuring more than a few publications and broadcasts can be unwieldy, particularly for beginning Trend Watchers. On the other hand, unduly limiting the media you track won't give you the breadth of coverage you need to get the full picture. The challenge, once again, is to obtain the most information with the least effort.

Divide the world of media into print (newspapers and periodicals) and electronic (TV and radio). Periodicals (magazines) should be further broken down into categories of general news, general business news, trade and professional news, and "precursors."

Think of the media-selection process as if you were George Gallup taking a poll. As any pollster knows, opinion polls are significant only when consisting of a representative sampling of the larger universe, so as to minimize potential for statistical error. So, too, must your media universe be representative for your Trend Watching to be as accurate as possible.

The media you use are determined in part by the universe of people involved in the issues you are tracking. This means your media must be those that reach and influence the group of people who are trendsetters, whether it be a profession, a segment of the consumer market, a geopolitical region, or the citizenry of an entire nation. Trendsetters are the actors in the sector in which you choose to work. Some may be more active than others, but you want to take into account as many in the total group as you can.

For many issues, trendsetters represent the entire U.S. populace, leading to the rather simple conclusion that your media sampling will be national in scope. (Exactly *which* national media you choose may require additional consideration, however.) If the universe of actors is too limited—smaller, say, than the population of a state or a large metropolitan area— it may be difficult to choose appropriate media whose area of influence matches the dispersion of influential, trendsetting people you want to track. (True, we are not tracking people *per se;* but trends are born of people and their actions.) In other words, to gain a measurable response, the trendsetters must be reached by a distinct set of media.

Your universe may be defined in a number of ways. It might be geographic—general marketing trends in the Midwest, for example—or it could be professional—physicians who are being affected by malpractice insurance costs throughout the country. It may be some combination of the two, such as trends in the sales of sporting goods in Texas. Whatever the universe, choose media that reach all the people in that universe and, ideally, *only* those people. In the perfect world, *Sporting Goods Texas*—should it exist—would be the ideal publication to track. Finding such a perfect publication on any subject would be rare, however. Even if it did exist, you would still want to know whether and how its stories are picked up by the general media, which affect the ultimate universe of those who buy sporting goods in the Lone Star State.

Distinguishing discrete universes can be difficult, and the differences can be subtle. The state of California, for example, represents a distinct geographic universe, while the state of New York does not. Why? Because Californians' media are relatively isolated; the *Los Angeles Times, San Jose Mercury, Sacramento Bee,* and *San Francisco Chronicle*'s readership and influence don't extend much beyond the state's borders. Similarly, television stations in California's major cities don't reach many people in adjoining states and, therefore, they focus their coverage on their in-state audiences.

New York media, in contrast, are located in the middle of the heavily populated eastern corridor and they cross many boundaries. New York newspapers and television stations reach —and are aimed at—audiences in New Jersey, Connecticut, Pennsylvania, even parts of Canada; in addition, media in those areas reach New Yorkers. The influence of some publications, most notably the *New York Times*, extends throughout the country, even overseas. Such overlaps make it difficult to isolate messages only New Yorkers are receiving. On the other hand, the media may be telling you something about the scope of your market. This is not to say that a media matrix cannot be drawn for New York state alone, if that's what you really want to cover, but don't overlook the fact that the media's boundaries often transcend geography.

If your area of Trend-Watching interest is highly specialized—attitudes of doctors toward prescribing contraceptive devices for birth control, for example—clearly you will want to focus primarily on professional publications, although the general media shouldn't be ignored altogether. Doctors, after all, are a portion, however small, of the overall population; as such, they are consumers of newspapers, television, and newsmagazines. Their professional practices—in this case, their tendency to prescribe birth-control methods—will be influenced to some degree by their perception of their patients' needs and fears. In that sense, they are Trend Watchers themselves.

The media-selection process needn't be cast in stone. You may find it necessary to fine-tune your Trend-Watching activities by adjusting your media mix, usually by adding new periodicals. Though you must make a change, it doesn't mean the information you've been getting isn't accurate. After all, prior to this you probably weren't tracking media in *any* organized fashion. The adjustment merely represents a sharpening of your focus, the removal of some slight imperfections in your Trend-Watching lens.

The National Media Index

Choosing media is a bit simpler if you are tracking national trends affecting a large segment of the population. We've already laid the groundwork for this by developing the National Media Index (NMI), more about which is in the Appendix. The NMI tracks the media that represent basic sources of news for most people in the United States. As a proxy for all national media, NMI uses the following to track several hundred subjects and subcategories: (1) the three television networks (ABC, CBS, and NBC); (2) the three national newsmagazines (*Newsweek*, *Time*, and *U.S. News & World Report*); and (3) five newspapers (*Chicago Tribune*, *Los Angeles Times*, *New York Times*, *Wall Street Journal*, and *Washington Post*).

In the National Media Index, these media are linked together by a weighted formula based on how Americans get their news on national issues. Television, for example, accounts for an average of 45 percent of the total, based on survey research done in the early 1980s by Robert P. Bower, formerly head of the Bureau of Social Sciences Research. When comparing television, newspaper, and magazine coverage, we weight each medium by a given figure, eliminating the "apples and oranges" comparison problem. We show precisely how to use this weighting system in Chapter Seven, including examples of real-life issues from the National Media Index.

Your Personal Index

Ultimately, you will most likely find it useful to devise a tailor-made group of publications and, when appropriate, television news shows. "The [your name here] Index" can reflect your specific perspective and interests. To do this, you will want to choose one or more from each of several categories:

1. *National publications.* These will be most helpful for getting the big picture—national trends. They include "local" newspapers and magazines whose reputations garner national audiences (primarily those mentioned as part of the National

Media Index). Their timeliness and their tendency to produce "trend" pieces, which pool the perspectives of reporters throughout the country, make them well suited for covering national trends affecting major segments of the population.

2. *Trade or business publications.* These are the key to your business interests. Mixing them into your Trend-Watching system, along with broader-scale media, automatically encourages you to look for relationships between seemingly dissimilar developments and to make the kinds of inferences that give value to the process.

3. *Local publications.* As you would expect, these are useful when tracking local and regional trends. They also serve as a secondary sampling to verify national findings on the local level. Perhaps their greatest importance is to spot grassroots movements. The notion that something must "play in Peoria"— or Pittsburgh, Pomona, or Petersborough—before it can become accepted nationally is one strong school of thought among Trend Watchers.

4. *Precursor publications.* As described in Chapter Four, these are publications whose expertise and authority influence other media or other influentials, and whose reports often become news stories themselves. Many such publications exist in the realm of science or technology: *New England Journal of Medicine, Science, Science News, Oil Daily,* and *Aviation Week* are several examples.

The Electronic Media

Television can be a very useful Trend-Watching medium, but only for certain kinds of issues. The principal advantage of television is that it is a general medium—"everybody" watches it—and its influential power is unequaled. A minute of television coverage can have the power of many column-inches in a magazine or newspaper.

When should you use television as part of your media sample? It can be most useful when you are covering issues that affect the overall population, whether it is local or national.

It is also most useful when you want to track local adaptation of broader national trends—if you want to see, for example, how an area leads or lags behind the overall population. Lastly, television is most helpful if you are dealing with trends related to consumer habits and generalized social behavior.

This last application is particularly worth noting. Television is a powerful marketing force, and news about consumer products and services—presented along with appeals to the marketplace through advertising—tend to reach people when they are in their consumer mode. Thanks to advertising, people are used to having their consumption habits influenced by television. Whether the influence comes from commercials or news stories is largely irrelevant. Because advertising is much less intrusive in newspapers (readers can skip through entire ad supplements without even opening them if they wish), its impact is far less linked to editorial content in the reader's mind. Magazines, for their part, fall somewhere in the middle. Their glossy, colorful ads can be real eye-grabbers. In the days before television, picture magazines like *Life* and *Look* served the function of linking content with ads; "As Advertised in *Life*" was as much an advertising slogan as was "The Pause That Refreshes."

Television may be at its best as a Trend-Watching instrument at the local level. There, topics from schools to sewers to shopping are heavily influenced by coverage on local television. Finally, this coverage is not always reflected in local print media, because many local television news production facilities are more sophisticated and extensive than those of local newspapers.

What about radio? As we've said, it's more difficult to measure, partly because radio generally has so many small news presentations during the broadcast day that it is hard to keep track of them. Besides, many of these newscasts originate nationally, making them less useful when tracking local trends. Moreover, it is difficult to be sure about the level of radio's exposure; people tend not to listen to the radio for extended periods, and they may change channels with great frequency. The result is that even the best ratings estimates are still only approximations, making it difficult for Trend Watchers to gauge the influence of a particular radio broadcast.

The problem of using either radio or television is that news stories on the electronic media are relatively difficult to store and keep track of. Unlike newspapers, which you could save in a pile and measure periodically at your convenience, television and radio stories must be measured as they happen. True, you can capture broadcasts on video- or audiotape, but this is an expensive proposition, particularly if you intend to cover more than one station at a time. One alternative are the services in most cities that provide written transcripts of broadcasts, but these can be quite expensive, particularly when attempting to ascertain the level of all coverage in a region for a given time period.

And then there is the problem of sheer quantity. In most cities, there are half a dozen or more television stations, a couple dozen radio stations, but only one or two major daily newspapers. This fact enhances the printed word's value as an accessible, widely seen, and easily measured medium.

Complementary Perspectives: Using Multiple Lenses

We spoke in Chapter Four about the need for a full perspective—a multilens approach—to avoid "driving with only one eye open." With Trend Watching, the ideal is use at least two "lenses" that will ensure your data are truly representative.

The two perspectives should be complementary. You could, for example, have a local lens and a national lens; or a current lens and a precursor lens. The specific lenses through which you want to view things will depend on the specific issue. Does the trend start with influential thinkers, like scientists, expressing themselves in professional journals? Such might be the case if, say, the owner of our gardening supply store wanted to know about new varieties of organic insecticides before they go on the market, in order to stay ahead of the competition. Or does the trend start on the local level, as seemingly disparate local events build momentum and take over nationally? That might be the case when determining how much news coverage is being given to—and, therefore, what the public perceives to be—the potential dangers of a hazardous pesticide. By comparing such local coverage with the pesticide coverage nationally, it might give the retailer a sense of the "local lag"—how long it takes before a national trend affects a local area—or "local lead"—how long it takes a local trend to spread to the national level.

An astute Trend Watcher would probably want to use a precursor lens and a local lens as well as the national one. But keep things simple. In a moment, when we describe shortcuts, you will be able to simplify the process so it won't be necessary to maintain three separate Trend-Watching systems.

Another type of multilens approach is to track media in several cities, a system similar to that used by John Naisbitt in *Megatrends*. This is very difficult, however. For one thing, it takes a certain amount of effort simply to obtain a dozen publications from different places on a regular basis. Inevitably, your information will be dated by the time it can be read, counted, and analyzed. And the period of coverage probably won't match exactly among the various publications.

The best solution is a compromise, using no more than two or three local newspapers and, wherever possible, supplementing them with regional periodicals—city or regional magazines, for example, like *Louisville* and *Texas Business*; or local weekly tabloids, such as the *Boston Phoenix* and Denver's *Westword*. But consider these regional and weekly publications as magazines in the weighting system we mention in Chapter Seven.

Media Mixes

It may be that your Trend-Watching interests are neither regional nor national, but somewhere in between: a cross section of a region and one or more industries, with a dash of national flavor thrown in for contrast. We've concocted a dozen different media mixes that may be of use to those with specialized interests. These dozen mixes are described in the pages that follow, divided into two major categories. Remember, though, that these are only samples. You can add to them, modify them, or create your own media mix.

Shortcuts for Specialists

There are several ways you can reduce the Trend-Watching burden to a more manageable size. One is to use fewer media as proxies for a larger number. This is risky, to be sure, but the time savings may make it worth it; at least you will know more than your competitors. Another way is to set up your system for the particular Trend-Watching values you are seeking. You may, for example, be interested strictly in the media's impact on markets and would, therefore, specialize in current general media like television. On the other hand, you may be really interested in predictions. If this is your principal concern, there is a special formula for you, too.

The following media mixes reflect some of the shortcuts you can take to maximize your Trend-Watching cost-benefit.

1. *The Minimalist.* This approach uses one or two print media and a short list of subjects to track. You can, for example, take the front page of the *Wall Street Journal*, where every major story gets at least a sentence or two. Do simple Trend Watching by counting the items day by day against a list of a couple dozen or so subjects. For example, counting the number of reports of increased earnings versus lower earnings among major companies—or companies within a specific sector—may provide sufficient insight on general economic trends. This is not unlike counting the raw number of help-wanted classifieds to monitor employment trends.

The *Wall Street Journal* is perfect for this service. It not only features a complete summary of issues important to business on one page, it also has some of the best investigative reporting in modern journalism. Almost no other American newspaper can afford the intensive investigation and editing given to the *Journal*'s full-length, front-page stories. These pose a peculiar problem for Trend Watchers because the *Journal* is such a powerful information force. Practically everyone in business reads the *Journal*, so it has little precursor value. Once the *Journal* has written a story, that's it; the trend emerges. It may not give you long-term forecasting ability, but the *Wall Street Journal* does have authority. If a news story emerges that's important, add it to your issues list and see how many additional instances of that subject occur.

For the small businessperson, there is probably no better single medium for Trend Watching than the *Journal*. Still, you might want to supplement it with *Business Week*, if your focus is strictly corporate, or with the *New York Times*, if you are oriented more toward social policy, international affairs, culture, or science. If you are interested strictly in consumer markets, you might add *USA Today*.

The Minimalist need not count column-inches to use this shortcut. The bad news is that counting so few media won't provide an accurate measure of exposure. The result is an overview of the recurrence of stories or "events." What the Minimalist gets, therefore, is a sense of movement in a fairly narrow area, simply by keeping a rough but rigorous count of things he or she would probably read every day. For an example of how this Minimalist approach might work for an investor, see Figure 6-1. The beginnings of trends in the economy are emerging, as are some signals about selected companies.

2. *The Prospector.* This approach uses a lot of magazines. Many Trend Watchers see the process as analogous to the '49ers' panning for gold. If you can get a nugget of truth about the future, you have found your treasure. If you're strictly seeking the pot of gold, this technique is for you. There is less value in rigorously measuring a broad swathe of general media, though they provide an excellent benchmark. For the Prospector, the gold will be found by digging out the precursor journals—those publications that influence your business, profession, customers, and other important actors in your field. As we have said before, some of these publications are so obvious that everyone already knows about them, but that doesn't mean they are not worth counting. But you can't focus

Figure 6-1 The Minimalist approach, as used by an investor.

News Category	Wall Street Journal				Business Week				Summary
	Week 1	Week 2	Total	×3	Week 1	Week 2	Total	×2	
ECONOMIC NEWS									
Positive	6	8	14	42	3	2	5	10	52
Negative	8	5	13	39	4	3	7	14	53
FEDERAL DEFICIT									
Spending	0	3	3	9	2	0	2	4	13
	1	0	1	3	0	1	1	2	5
MONEY ISSUES									
Dollar	16	19	35	105	6	9	15	30	135
Inflation	3	2	5	15	0	0	0	0	15
Interest rates	2	5	7	21	2	2	4	8	29
Institutions	1	4	5	15	2	1	3	6	21
Other	7	6	13	39	2	6	8	16	55
	3	2	5	15	0	0	0	0	15
CORPORATE PERFORMANCE									
Computer Companies:									
IBM positive	7	3	10	30	0	2	2	4	36
negative	2	1	3	9	0	1	1	2	11
Apple positive	0	0	0	0	0	1	1	2	2
negative	3	1	4	12	0	0	0	0	12
negative	0	0	0	0	0	0	0	0	0
Automobiles:									
GM positive	0	1	1	3	0	0	0	0	3
negative	3	0	3	9	0	0	0	0	9
Ford positive	0	1	1	3	0	0	0	0	3
negative	0	0	0	0	0	0	0	0	0
All others	0	2	2	6	1	1	2	4	10
TRADE									
With Japan	7	6	13	39	4	2	6	12	51
	3	3	6	18	2	0	2	4	22
TAKEOVERS	10	10	20	60	2	1	3	6	66

just on these, lest you simply gain the same knowledge as everyone else.

The risk in this approach is in making your focus too narrow, thus missing important countertrends and themes that are building in the economy and that will strongly influence the technical changes you have spotted. One of the real benefits of Trend Watching is to be able to put into perspective some of the predictions others are making about change. This usually happens in a technical area; for example, it has been freely predicted that everyone will soon be using car telephones, though in fact, the trends toward auto safety and privacy are working strongly against it.

3. *The Specialist*. This approach uses trade magazines, the front page of the *Wall Street Journal*, and a technical precursor publication. For those who want a tailor-made shortcut, a combination of publications that bring together your field of interest with a broader range of news—and perhaps some perspective on scientific or technological change—may fill the bill. The idea is to encompass the entire range of meaningful information using the fewest possible media. This differs from the Minimalist approach in that, rather than relying entirely on one or two publications, you are covering most or all of the bases.

Again, you will rely on the *Wall Street Journal* as the basic medium—even as a source of international and political news to the extent you need to know about that. Add to this one or two relevant trade publications and a good scientific magazine to expand your horizon. If you need a marketing perspective, you will want to know a bit more about consumer attitudes; television or *USA Today* (which is sometimes referred to as "daytime television for literates") may be helpful. The advantages of supplementing the *Journal* with *USA Today* is that you get a fairly broad perspective of what's happening in the country as a whole. And, if you use the two together, you'll have sufficient material to make some reasonably reliable measurements of exposure. Otherwise, this mixture will have to be treated as the two other approaches just mentioned—strictly as a matter of counting articles, but not of measuring them.

4. *The Regionalist.* This approach includes one major regional paper along with or in addition to a series of city or regional magazines and a newspaper from a state capital. Many businesses aren't national in scope but have broad market areas stretching over several states. Anyone familiar with advertising and marketing knows about matching media with market area. The Regionalist approach does precisely this, and spots trends at the same time.

If you are a manufacturer in the Midwest with a market area streaming west of Chicago, your first pick would probably be the *Chicago Tribune,* which has a strong regional influence. If your market is centered on one or two particular states, you may wish to add dailies from nearby state capitals: the *Des Moines (Iowa) Register, Lincoln (Nebraska) Journal,* or the *Wisconsin State Journal,* published in Madison. The advantage of state capital papers is that they can provide up-to-date information on changes in regulation and policy affecting your business. Local magazines—*Chicago, Crain's Chicago Business, Milwaukee, St. Louis,* or *St. Louis Business Journal,* for example—will provide a base of information on regional developments, both political and market.

The weakness in the regional approach is that while market areas may seem to be tight little islands, the minds of the island dwellers are strongly affected by the national media, particularly television and, increasingly, from outside the United States. The strength of the Regionalist approach is that you can get closer to grassroots change.

5. *The Partialist.* This approach combines the front page of the *Wall Street Journal,* the *New York Times* index, and a scan of local papers. Many Trend Watchers face the dilemma of how to balance local and national influences to get a multilens approach without counting a huge number of publications. The answer can be found in doing only part of the job. The trick is to scan major national publications on an article-by-article basis using indexes or, in the case of the *Wall Street Journal,* the front page. In this way, you can keep up with national change. The beauty of this approach is that the material can be more easily clipped and filed; the regularly published

New York Times index, in fact, can serve as a standard reference for Trend Watchers.

To this system should be added some fairly intensive counting and measuring of local newspapers—at least two, preferably three—from regions of interest to you. This won't give you a local basis on which to make national extrapolations, but it will provide a feel for one or more key regions. It is very important to select the right local papers, not ones that are competing on the national level. For example, the *Atlanta Constitution* and *St. Louis Post-Dispatch* are great papers, but their outlook is pronouncedly outward. What you're looking for is the local touch, which might be better found in the *Peoria Journal* (if you want to know what's playing there) or the *Fresno Bee*. The local papers to avoid are those owned by national chains, such as the *Denver Post* (owned by MediaNews Group) or the *San Antonio Light* (owned by Hearst Publications)—unless, of course, your interests lie in either of those regions.

6. *The Media Maven.* This approach uses national newsmagazines, the *New York Times*, and the *Wall Street Journal.* Trend Watching is media watching, and for many that is its primary purpose. If your focus is markets, you want to know how the media are treating key issues that might affect advertising or consumer values. For this purpose, there is often no substitute for television. However, because network news broadcasts are very often derived from precursor work done by the major national press, particularly the *New York Times*, it is possible to take a shortcut. This still requires counting and measuring, since there is no alternative to getting an exposure reading if your objective is to see how the media themselves are evaluating information flows. What you are measuring with this approach is the judgment of editors and how they fill the news hole.

This shortcut really depends on the three national newsmagazines—*Time, Newsweek*, and *U.S. News & World Report*—which are concise, easy to count, and locked in a long-run fight for survival against television and each other. In the Media

Maven, we simply make them a proxy for television and weigh the magazines against the newspapers accordingly.

Zeroing In

All of the approaches just described are shortcuts to getting the big picture. But what if you want to zero in on a specific part of the picture? There are ways to organize material to suit your special interests. Below are more focused approaches that may suit some specific needs. Use them as is or as guides to building your own version.

7. *The Financier.* This focuses on financial matters. For those whose primary concern is to manage money or to follow the links between financial markets and individual firms or industries, there are several obvious media that must be scanned carefully: *Business Week,* the *Wall Street Journal, Barron's,* and the *Wall Street Transcript,* among others. The simplest approach is to cover the *Journal* plus at least one other of these publications. To this mix add a dash of special interests—a trade magazine, perhaps, or an international market pacer like the London-based *Financial Times,* if your interests transcend international borders. One of the beauties of scanning the financial markets is that television has so little direct relevance here; your news hole can consist entirely of printed matter.

Smart financial analysts already read this material, of course, and much more, including the insider market letters. There is no reason why such material can't be added as precursor publications, if you have faith in a particular service. "Faith," in this case, is up to you; if you have tested a particular analyst, Trend Watching can serve the valuable purpose of keeping that analyst honest.

But the main purpose here is to reduce to a fairly rigorous discipline the vast amount of financial material that thousands of others have already read. By developing a set of trend data, you can build your own analytical tool that may help you get an edge on competitors. Again, because time literally is money in the financial market, speed is of the essence. Use a computer.

8. *The Elitist.* This method uses such high-brow publications as *Atlantic, New Yorker, Foreign Affairs, Commentary, Economist, New York Review of Books,* and public broadcasting's "McNeil-Lehrer Report." For the individual whose interest is matters of policy and who feels a need to see the world holistically, there is a ready-made array of established media that over the years have moved America's elites. Some, like *Foreign Affairs,* may seem a little stodgy and can be replaced, if desired, with more activist material like *Foreign Policy.* Other publications—the *New York Review of Books,* for example— draw their strength from a willingness to confront new ideas and, as a result, constantly pose new intellectual challenges. For the Elitist, there is a dilemma between concentrating on what "in" groups know now, already "trendy" at the mass level, and what they will be talking about in the future. This, of course, is the whole point of Trend Watching: to look beyond what's "in" now to the future. Therefore, the mix should include more of the provocative publications (*New York Review of Books, Atlantic*) and less of the orthodox (*Foreign Affairs, Economist*). The important thing is to have a wide scope, including as many periodicals as you can handle. Add a bit of spice in the form of periodicals that cover science, art, literature, and philosophy.

Again, the value of this approach is that you will get an idea of the directions in which leading thinkers are moving. This does not require that you be any great genius yourself; it is simply one way to deal with the daunting problem of keeping up with the intellectual elites.

9. *The Extremist.* This method uses right- and left-wing publications like *National Review, Human Events, Progressive,* and *Mother Jones.* If you are an issues manager in an organization worried about demonstrations at the front gate, labor demands, consumer activism, or demands for regulatory or social reform, you will want to stay on top of society's extreme political and social thinking. (In America, today's extremes have a curious way of becoming tomorrow's convention.) This is fairly simple to do. There is a sizable pool of periodical literature which you can peruse. The design of your sampling

will be something like a Chinese menu: two from column A, two from column B, perhaps a few exotic delicacies of your own choosing. Take a couple from the right (*National Review, Human Events*), perhaps a Christian conservative (such as *Plain Truth*), and a couple from the left (*Progressive, The Nation*). To these, add a sampling of the alternative press. This can be done very simply by subscribing to *Utne Reader*, a monthly digest of alternative and trendy ideas.

10. *The Entertainer*. This uses *Variety, Hollywood Reporter,* and the entertainment sections of the *New York Times* and the *Los Angeles Times.* For those who want to follow entertainment, there's no substitute for these publications. If you haven't looked at *Variety* lately and you have become aware of information age thinking, you're in for a big surprise. *Variety* has become the best source of information on penetration of U.S. television outside the country. It is truly an information age publication, as any entertainment periodical should be. We are, after all, in an age of "info-tainment," in which the lines between information and entertainment have become as fuzzy as Dan Rather's sweaters. But before attempting the arduous task of counting the themes in each week's episodes of "Dallas," "Cosby," or any other show, you'll find it considerably more efficient to get behind the scenes, as it were.

With the rise of "info-tainment"—and the need of the news media to sell their wares—this area has become one of the most exciting Trend Watching frontiers. There can be great value in examining this group of periodicals. It can provide lead themes for changes in social behavior because it gives clues to their future exposure en masse. It can also help sort out what is pure entertainment from what is truly news. The links between *Rambo* and reality are becoming increasingly— and frighteningly—close.

11. *The Globalist*. This approach uses such international sources as *Economist, World Press Review, Far Eastern Economic Review*, the *International Herald Tribune*, and *South* magazine. Increasingly, as we've said, there is a trend toward greater foreign influence in the way America—or any other country—does business. You needn't learn exotic languages to

find these trends; there is plenty of material in English. The main point is to get soundings from every corner of the globe. The Globalist, by definition, must look at the world as a whole. This is not a question of emphasizing particular regions—Asia, for example, or the Middle East—but of looking at major worldwide trends. The selection you use should probably begin with the *Economist* and *World Press Review* to ensure getting news directly from overseas (as opposed to through the American news filter). For balance, add the *New York Times*, which has the broadest foreign coverage of any American media; then add regional periodicals like *Far Eastern Economic Review* and *South* magazine, which covers Latin America.

Beware of the pitfall of converting an American point of view to a British one. Much of the really good international news originates from London although, like *South* magazine, it is edited by journalists coming from and trained in the Third World. There is also a vast number of newsletters and periodicals on foreign affairs originating in the United States, many of which are of equal quality. There is no substitute, however, for the *New York Times*, unless you desire a Euro-American point of view and can gain regular access to the *International Herald Tribune*. Another possibility is to examine Canadian material, particularly the *Toronto Globe and Mail*, which has a very different, though still North American, outlook.

12. *The Sensationalist*. This last approach uses the *National Enquirer*, *People* magazine, *GQ*, *Esquire*, *W*, and the newsweekly of your choice. Much of America thrives on images. These are usually not indicators of trends to come, but of trends that are or were. The Sensationalist approach, therefore, is for the individual who wants to know what's going on in a very trendy and materialistic way—fashion designers or marketers, for example, or retailers whose business depends largely on constantly shifting public tastes. Most of these publications will be "trendy," but the newsmagazine is added for balance and as a baseline to sanity: To determine just how zany and bizarre a bit of news is, it's necessary to have a context in which it can be measured. This is a minor adaptation of the multilens approach discussed in Chapter Five.

It is literally true that there are clues to public behavior in the report that a movie star attended the wedding of a space alien and an Elvis clone. Those truths are that the Elvis myth, with all its market importance, continues to grow; that aliens are still "in"; and that image-conscious movie stars are willing to participate in such nonsense. The fact that there is a market for such sensationalism indicates that this is an important part of what the public needs to know. By Trend-Watching definition, that's "news."

The Ideal Mix

Ultimately, the ideal media mix should consist of the following:

- Two or three newspapers, of which one might be national.
- Several general or specialized magazines, depending on the nature of the issue. Magazines are the easiest things to count, so don't hesitate to use them; the more, the merrier.
- At least two television news programs, preferably local programs, for anyone dealing with consumer issues. If the focus of the Trend Watching is strictly business, however, you may be able to get by without television at all, saving you the time and trouble of keeping accurate tabs.

You've now selected your issues and the media you will monitor to track them. Don't be concerned if the fit between issues and media doesn't seem ideal. Here are three tips to keep in mind:

1. Never subtract from an issues list, only add. By deleting issues, you may be losing sight of something that was once—and may again someday be—significant.
2. Avoid dropping media from your mix; you are better off adding. You are only enriching the media mix and

ensuring that your coverage is comparable from one
time period to the next.
3. Organize your issues into sets and subsets. This will help
   make monitoring manageable and will ensure that things
   don't get counted twice.

Ultimately, you simply can't *read* everything, but you can *scan*,
count, and *analyze* a surprising amount of material. Trend
Watching, as we've said, actually permits you to cover more
material in less time.

By now, you've really made the toughest decisions in the
Trend-Watching process. Now it is time to start counting.

7

Counting and Calculating

This is the easiest but most tedious part of Trend Watching. You'll be relying on some basic arithmetic skills, although we'll help you with some simple formulas along the way.

Determining the News Hole

The first step in counting the news you've been tracking is to determine the size of each medium's news hole. This is a simple math problem, although there are some important considerations. The idea is to determine the amount of space or time each publication or program devotes to news—the actual news stories, minus the advertisements and commercials. But you won't be counting *all* news stories.

There is a slight difference in the approach to calculating the news hole for print media and television.

Print Media

When tracking most issues in a newspaper or magazine, you will want to use only the major news sections of the publications you are monitoring: the National, International, Business, and, for local issues, the Metro section. Some issues— gardening, for example—might lead you to the Women's Pages or Style sections, or the Leisure or Hobby sections. You should also count photographs and other illustrations, including captions and headlines. Except for very special cases, do not count sports, classified ads, weather, obituaries, comics, puzzles, events listings, personality columns, or local or syndicated humor or advice columnists, such as those by Ann Landers, Abigail Van Buren, Art Buchwald, Erma Bombeck, Russell Baker, Bob Greene, among many others. (We by no means intend to denigrate the work of these scribes, many of whom have sterling reputations and devoted followings. Using their columns for Trend-Watching purposes is extremely difficult, however, and probably more trouble than it is worth.) Don't count advertisements.

When measuring publications, you are counting inches, specifically column-inches. A column-inch is a linear inch of a column in a publication. A newspaper typically has five to seven columns on a page, although papers sometimes have double-width columns for features stories that must be factored in during your count. The *Washington Post*, for example, typically has 132 column-inches on each full page of its main news sections (six columns per page times 22 inches per column); the *New York Times* has 123 column-inches (six columns times 20½ inches). But certain news sections—particularly in the Sunday editions of both papers—use different column configurations, sometimes as few as two columns per page.

Because the size of most newspapers varies from day to day owing primarily to the amount of advertising, try to obtain a seasonal average of each publication's total news hole. Newspapers and magazines tend to be larger near Christmas and to shrink during the summer, for example (not including the larger editions that accompany sale ads for the Fourth of July, Labor Day, and other holidays). Because the news hole will remain constant for Trend-Watching purposes, it is to your advantage to get the most accurate number possible. To be most accurate, go to your public library and use 20 to 25 editions spaced throughout the year to calculate an average. Add up the total number of column-inches and divide by the number of newspapers you've measured. If, for example, the total number of column-inches for 20 issues of a given paper equals 90,000, the paper has an average news hole of 4,500 column-inches (90,000 divided by 20). That's the total news hole, and it will become a standard measurement of your Trend-Watching activities.

Television

A television news hole is easier to calculate. It is simply the number of minutes of a broadcast—typically thirty minutes or an hour—minus the number of minutes of commercials. (Because television stations must maintain a record of commercial time, you can call a station to get this information.) A half-hour news broadcast typically has 22 or 23 minutes of actual "news," although if you are measuring local news, eliminate the time devoted to sports and weather stories unless they somehow relate to your topic of interest.

The Counting Process

Who in your company should do the counting? Almost anyone. Keep in mind that the counting process can be delegated. It's an ideal task for the homebound and the handicapped, among many others, because it's fairly interesting work and gives meaning to what people can do if their activity is restricted. You, or whoever is in charge, should count at least one publication or program yourself to get the "smell" of the news, a feeling for how the process works. A business paper is the most logical thing to count for this purpose.

How to Count

Each counter should have one sheet for each day's publication or program. The counter lays a ruler down the column and counts the length of each story in column-inches, including headlines, pictures, and captions. Don't make any special allotments for the front page; these stories tend to be longer anyway so their weight is felt by their sheer volume. The counting sheet will show the subject or issue and the number of column-inches or broadcast-minutes and seconds.

The question invariably arises: Can one story cover more than one subject? Usually the answer is no, because journalists tend to write with clarity of theme and, while there may be subissues from that theme, stories rarely carry more than one major theme. By double-counting one story in two or more categories, you will show more coverage than has actually appeared, skewing your results all the way down the line. This is where your judgment—and your willingness to stick to your decisions—counts most. Remember that what you are trying to do is compare coverage over time, not simply draw raw aggregates.

There are exceptions, however. Some stories are poorly edited, with two or more themes getting through. And there are round-up stories and those reporting on press conferences or meetings in which a litany of subjects may be covered. At most newspapers the reporter and the headline writer are two different people, so the headline and the story sometimes disagree, dealing with two different subjects or two different perspectives of the same subject. In such cases, count both the headline and the story, alloting the appropriate column-inches to each.

When counting column-inches, simplify things by knowing the length of each publication's full column. If you know a column is, say 22 inches, and a story covers about two and a half columns, you can simply write down "55 inches," without having to use a ruler.

When counting broadcast-minutes, there is no getting around using a stopwatch. Don't bother with increments of less than ten seconds (you'll be surprised how many stories are less than ten seconds). You're dealing with approximations here, trying to show what portion of the news capacity in each medium is given to a subject.

Inevitably, your figures won't agree with those of an editor—or, perhaps, other Trend Watchers, each of whom may have a slightly different count. The key is to be consistent, counting each broadcast and each publication the same way every day.

How to Track Key Events

While you are doing your counting, keep a separate list of key events going on in the world, although not necessarily every event every day. This will become an "event line," a calendar showing one or two major news stories each day. (In fact, you may wish to use a calendar for this purpose.) This event line will give you an idea of what major stories are moving the news, as distinguished from longer-term influences. Figure 7-1 is an example of an event line showing how social issues rose steadily during the designated time period. It also marks the beginning and ebbs and flows of the Iran-contra affair that dominated the national news during this period.

When to Count

Should you count every day? As a businessperson, you probably can get by on a five-day business week, excluding weekends. On the other hand, you should make allowances for the in-depth features that appear in the Sunday editions of many metropolitan dailies. This isn't true for television news, which brings in its second-string reporters and anchors on weekends. You can omit weekend television coverage, barring special events.

Ultimately, a complete batch of data will consist of a week's worth of counting, with one page per publication or program per day showing raw numbers of column-inches or broadcast-minutes and seconds, together with your event line of key events.

The Calculations

Now that you've done the raw counting, the next step is to make some calculations, which you should do on a weekly basis. We assume that you will be doing this by hand, although the job could be set up on a simple spreadsheet or data base computer program, if you are so inclined.

The calculation process consists of the following steps:

- Add up all the numbers by issue and by medium
- Convert the numbers to percentages
- Derive the percentages for each medium
- Crunch the numbers

We'll take it a step at a time.

1. *Add up all the numbers by issue and by medium.* The results of this will be one sheet for, say, the *Los Angeles Times*, for each week. Down the left-hand side of the page is your list of issues; across the top is the day-by-day summary. In the grid thus formed are each day's counts. On the right-hand side of the page are weekly totals for each issue. Figure 7-2 is an example of a typical daily count sheet.

2. *Convert the numbers to percentages.* At the end of each week, convert the count to percentages. You must convert each publication's or each program's coverage on each issue to a common denominator, which in this case is a percentage of the news hole. For example, if a newspaper's news hole for a given week is 5,000 column-inches, and the coverage of a particular subject you are tracking totals 250 column-inches, that subject rates 5 percent of the news hole. Your end product will be a series of percentages in the right-hand vertical column for each issue on each weekly media sheet. Figure 7-3 shows these percentages as they relate to the daily count sheet shown in Figure 7-2.

(text continued on p. 126)

Figure 7-1 Event line showing major news topics, November 1985–April 1986.

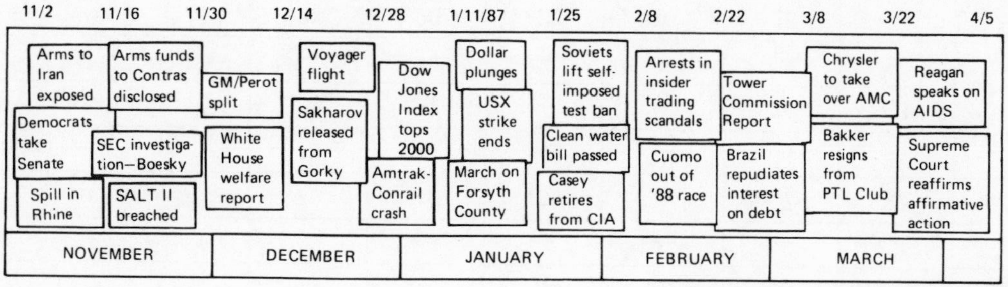

11/2	11/16	11/30	12/14	12/28	1/11/87	1/25	2/8	2/22	3/8	3/22	4/5

Arms to Iran exposed

Arms funds to Contras disclosed

GM/Perot split

Voyager flight

Dow Jones Index tops 2000

Dollar plunges

Soviets lift self-imposed test ban

Arrests in insider trading scandals

Tower Commission Report

Chrysler to take over AMC

Reagan speaks on AIDS

Democrats take Senate

SEC investigation—Boesky

White House welfare report

Sakharov released from Gorky

USX strike ends

Clean water bill passed

Cuomo out of '88 race

Brazil repudiates interest on debt

Bakker resigns from PTL Club

Supreme Court reaffirms affirmative action

Spill in Rhine

SALT II breached

Amtrak-Conrail crash

March on Forsyth County

Casey retires from CIA

NOVEMBER	DECEMBER	JANUARY	FEBRUARY	MARCH	

Note: Media coverage was tracked in two-week periods.

Figure 7-2 Daily count sheet: *Los Angeles Times*, March 1–7.

Issues	Day 1	Day 2	Day 3	Day 4	Day 5	Day 6	Day 7	Total
Negative economic news	41	14	18	—	—	11	28	112
Positive economic news	—	18	13	24	16	—	—	71
Labor	—	—	24	10	15	—	—	49
Wages	—	—	—	—	—	—	—	—
Trade	70	40	106	—	7	27	51	301
Agricultural	15	—	42	—	—	—	21	78
Regulatory legislation	36	32	—	—	26	63	24	181
FDA	—	14	—	—	26	50	24	114
Health	31	20	138	70	28	—	49	336
Insurance	10	—	98	—	—	—	—	108
Environment	23	70	36	17	—	10	121	277
Drug abuse	12	18	20	—	18	—	—	68
On the job	—	18	—	—	—	—	—	18

Note: Issues measured in column-inches.

Figure 7-3 News hole percentages for the *Los Angeles Times*, March 1–7.

Issues	Day 1	Day 2	Day 3	Day 4	Day 5	Day 6	Day 7	Total	Percent of News Hole
Negative economic news	41	14	18	—	—	11	28	112	2.24
Positive economic news	—	18	13	24	16	—	—	71	1.42
Labor	—	—	24	10	15	—	—	49	.98
Wages	—	—	—	—	—	—	—	—	—
Trade	70	40	106	—	7	27	51	301	6.02
Agricultural	15	—	42	—	—	—	21	78	1.56
Regulatory legislation	36	32	—	—	26	63	24	181	3.62
FDA	—	14	—	—	26	50	24	114	2.28
Health	31	20	138	70	28	—	49	336	6.72
Insurance	10	—	98	—	—	—	—	108	2.16
Environment	23	70	36	17	—	10	121	277	5.54
Drug Abuse	12	18	20	—	18	—	—	68	1.36
On the job	—	18	—	—	—	—	—	18	.36

Note: Percentages measured in column-inches, based on estimated news hole of 5,000 column-inches per week.

Figure 7-4 Weekly news hole percentages for three leading newspapers.

Issues	Los Angeles Times	Chicago Tribune	New York Times	Total	Average
Negative economic news	2.24	7.89	1.82	11.95	3.98
Positive economic news	1.42	1.81	1.43	4.66	1.55
Labor	.98	2.67	1.50	5.15	1.72
Wages	—	.37	.41	.78	.26
Trade	6.02	5.41	3.60	15.03	5.03
Agricultural	1.56	.43	.18	2.17	.72
Regulatory legislation	3.62	2.16	4.07	9.85	3.28
FDA	2.28	1.84	2.29	6.41	2.14
Health	6.72	4.83	9.42	20.97	6.99
Insurance	2.16	.56	1.41	4.13	1.38
Environment	5.54	4.74	2.61	12.89	4.30
Drug Abuse	1.36	2.67	1.47	5.50	1.83
On the job	.36	1.07	.44	1.87	.62

Note: Percentages measured in column-inches.

Figure 7-5 Summary percentages for media news holes, by type of media.

Issues	Television		Newspapers		Magazines		Percent of Total Media Index
	Percent of News Hole	× .5	Percent of News Hole	× .3	Percent of News Hole	× .2	
Negative economic news	0.63	.32	3.98	1.19	1.67	.33	1.84
Positive economic news	.06	.03	1.55	.47	.33	.07	.57
Labor	1.13	.57	1.72	.52	1.22	.24	1.33
Wages	—	—	.26	.08	.55	.11	.19
Trade	1.12	.56	5.03	1.51	4.11	.82	2.89
Agricultural	—	—	.72	.22	1.11	.22	.44
Regulatory legislation	1.31	.66	3.28	.98	1.11	.22	1.86
FDA	1.31	.66	2.14	.64	1.11	.22	1.52
Health	5.48	2.74	6.99	2.10	13.44	2.69	7.53
Insurance	.45	.23	1.38	.41	1.11	.22	.86
Environment	1.83	.92	4.30	1.29	.33	.07	2.28
Drug Abuse	.97	.49	1.83	.55	—	—	1.04
On the job	—	—	.62	.19	—	—	.19

3. *Derive the percentages for each medium.* You need to combine like media—television with television, newspapers with newspapers, and so on—to get aggregate totals for each media category. Set up a grid week showing in each week on a single page so you can keep at least one quarter's data (13 weeks) together for each issue you're tracking. Using still another grid, combine all the newspaper coverage onto one sheet, all the television coverage onto another, and all the magazine coverage on yet another. If you are using two newspapers, and one gave 10 percent of its coverage to a subject and the other gave 6 percent to the same subject, the average will be 8 percent of all newspaper coverage for that period. Figure 7-4 shows how the total news hole percentages for newspapers have been assembled, giving a total and an average for each of the surveyed topics. If you were monitoring television and newsmagazines on these same issues, you would have separate percentage sheets for those two media.

4. *Crunch the numbers.* This step involves linking newspapers, magazines, and television coverage into a single index. To effectively combine apples and oranges, it is necessary to weight each medium's coverage, based on what survey research has told us how Americans get their news.

For national news, according to all research, television carries considerably more weight than the print media. However, that weight decreases with an audience's level of education. For Americans who have reached college, research shows the following rough weighting:

television: 5
newspapers: 3
magazines: 2

This weighting means that 1 percent of total television exposure has 60 percent more influence than 1 percent of newspaper coverage and 150 percent more influence than the same percentage of magazine coverage. (If you want to spend the money, your own survey research will likely yield slightly different calculations, but for a national average the 5-3-2 ratio has proved a consistently effective weighting system.)

To "crunch" the numbers as a computer would do, take a final sheet with the issues listed and calculate the index number for that period. This is the magic number that represents the percentage of the news hole for each subject you are following, for the set of media you have chosen for a given period. Figure 7-5 is an example of such a summary showing the percentage of news hole for each of the issues for each of the media. Note that the right-hand column gives the percentage of total media coverage for each issue.

You should crunch your data at least every two weeks. The numbers you get are the basic building blocks you will use to construct your trend lines. Of course, the numbers don't explain everything. There are, from time to time, unexpected reasons why a particular story received high or low coverage. In Chapter Eight we show how to plot your numbers against the event lines described earlier in this chapter to show media sensitivity to developing events. Then you can compare your numbers with other trend information to see how trends compete with one another.

You should be aware, however, that there will be instances when precursor articles—exciting discoveries, provocative new ideas, and sensational speeches—have an intrinsic value as a source of information leading to later change. They may be small in measured exposure, but they will be large in trend potential. Nothing you do with numbers should dull your eye for such material. If you think you have spotted such an item, the idea or subject should at once be entered into your issues list as an appropriate subset so you can follow its development. If you are watching insurance liability problems, for example, and an article appears about a new kind of approach to the courts, flag that as a separate issue or subset of the main issue being watched.

It is important to keep in mind that this whole Trend-Watching system, for all its numbers, remains somewhat subjective. The numbers are merely guidelines—a means for approximating and measuring the appearance of certain kinds of information in the total flow. Trend Watching is intended not so much to give answers as to lead you in useful directions and force you to ask the right questions. But you can't ask these vital questions, or even make educated guesses, without good numbers. In the final step of the Trend-Watching process—analyzing the results and making predictions—the fruits of your careful number-crunching labors will readily become apparent.

8

Analyzing and Predicting

As a result of your crunched numbers, you will be able to do two things. First, you'll be able to plot graphs reflecting changes in the coverage of the subjects you've been tracking. These graphs, like Figure 8-1, will help you see the relationships you must understand to gain the benefits of Trend Watching. In Figure 8-1, you can see clearly: (1) how media coverage of health issues rose to become a substantial news flow during the mid-1980s; (2) how relatively little of this coverage was focused on cost; and (3) the rapid rise in concern over AIDS. Each of these factors tells you about key relationships in society. They show, for example, that health was already a big and growing factor in media coverage before AIDS really got a lot of attention, and that in spite of concern about rising costs, there was much more attention paid to health care needs.

Second, you should be able to begin asking some questions about your areas of interest. For example:

1. Why has coverage of some subjects risen or fallen?
2. What results seem surprising?
3. What subjects seem to have small but unfailingly steady media coverage?

Figure 8-1 Coverage of health issues in the national media, 1984–1986.

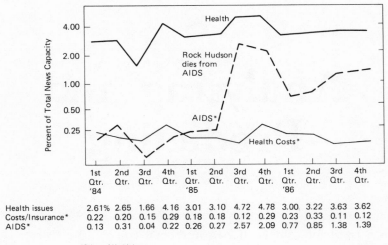

	1st Qtr. '84	2nd Qtr.	3rd Qtr.	4th Qtr.	1st Qtr. '85	2nd Qtr.	3rd Qtr.	4th Qtr.	1st Qtr. '86	2nd Qtr.	3rd Qtr.	4th Qtr.
Health issues	2.61%	2.65	1.66	4.16	3.01	3.10	4.72	4.78	3.00	3.22	3.63	3.62
Costs/Insurance*	0.22	0.20	0.15	0.29	0.18	0.18	0.12	0.29	0.23	0.33	0.11	0.12
AIDS*	0.13	0.31	0.04	0.22	0.26	0.27	2.57	2.09	0.77	0.85	1.38	1.39

*Subset of Health Issues.

4. Does coverage of some subjects rise at the same time that coverage of others falls?

The answers to these questions will give you your first "trends." By compiling a list of subjects from week to week, and plotting and comparing these lists over time, you'll obtain some basic information about what subjects are rising and falling in media coverage. Sophisticated analysis notwithstanding, there's no substitute for simply looking at the numbers to see how different issues compare. The key is consistency: consistent weekly tracking, record keeping, number crunching, and summaries.

Reading the Numbers

You will learn that merely looking at numbers can give you clues even before you draw a graph. For example, try looking at the same information in Figure 8-1, presented as numbers in sequence. For some people, numbers are not easy to use. For you who can use them, they will save a lot of time, and you can direct more effort toward looking at the whole of your universe of data, simply by eyeballing your count sheets.

For example, you may see that the environment consistently gets 1.8 percent of all media coverage, week in and week out. (This is a real statistic; since 1980, environmental coverage in the United States has remained between 1.5 percent and 2 percent.) As you continue your media tracking over weeks and months, you will become accustomed to the relative role of various issues, themes, and subjects, and you will become more sensitive to changes in their levels of coverage.

Those consistent levels are important (as we stated earlier, small but steady coverage over time can bring change) but you are really looking for improbabilities—changes in coverage that have no immediate explanation. These are the precursors of trends, the smoke signals that tell you something is going on. Why has coverage of white collar crime dropped for the past month? Is it Christmas, with reporters turning to other, happier stories? Or have business reporters gone off skiing in Vail? It may have a simple answer, but you'll never know unless you ask the question. A large part of Trend Watching involves crying "Wolf!"—looking suspiciously at issues that may turn out to have no real significance. Occasionally, one of them does have significance, and you'll be ahead of the pack.

This process of spotting change will be made easier through the use of graphs, on which you can draw trend lines. A computer may help here, but a simple, low-tech piece of graph paper can do just fine. We've provided a wealth of examples in Chapter Nine.

Keep in mind that every set of numbers will not reveal a trend in the time frame you are looking at. Often, numbers may zigzag up and down with no consistent pattern. Nevertheless, each set of numbers is significant because it gives the score for that point in time, for a given subject's ability to compete for attention in the media—and, therefore, to compete for attention in the public's mind. Bear in mind constantly that all issues compete with each other for space and time in the news hole. Events of each day will have an enormous effect on each subject's coverage over time; its path on your graph may be very bumpy. Certain kinds of crime stories, such as hijackings, are generally written about only when they take place, for example. But even coverage of such event-driven subjects as crime can vary, as reporters perceive a rising or falling interest; a hijacking that would have made front-page news last year may be so commonplace this year as to rate only three paragraphs on page six.

If you have chosen your topics well—if you have defined them in terms of the themes, images, and issues you are looking for—you will be amazed at how relatively smooth the path of change in coverage is from one period to the next. You are penetrating the veil of events to get at the reality of what the news is telling the public. In other words, you are looking at the substantial force of the news, rather than at a chronology of events.

This whole process isn't different from what you do naturally. As you follow news—consciously or subliminally—you get a sense of "what's going on." As a new subject seems to gain the limelight you think, "Hey, this is different. It's a change from the status quo." But Trend Watching gives you enormous leverage by showing you the volume of exposure, how issues compete, and what issue is getting media attention and what is not. It methodically measures and compares the effects of these impulses, not just for an individual, but for the mass of society.

Measuring Exposure

By simply measuring raw exposure for a subject, you can elicit clues to trend development; the public doesn't forget what it's been told. Consequently, individuals' memories build over time. That memory may be influenced by the negative or positive nature of the coverage and by other factors, but the memory builds nonetheless. It is possible to foresee how future events will play out against what the public already knows.

This is a phenomenon well known by politicians. Take drug abuse, for example. In 1986, the public became bombarded with coverage of drugs and drug abuse, in part owing to the advent of a potent form of cocaine called "crack." Politicians were quick to catch the wave of public interest on this subject, falling over each other to do things that would help the public identify them with this pressing issue. (It didn't hurt that 1986 was a national election year, and both parties were desperate for issues to claim as their own.) Simultaneously, small but significant segments of the population who continued to argue and lobby—sometimes persuasively—about such things as the legalization of marijuana or about issues related to drug treatment, were virtually shut out of the action. No politician, in the wake of this media blitz, would dare stand against the current.

This was extremely predictable. Why? Because of the rapid buildup of media coverage of crack and drug abuse throughout the country during a few months of 1986, which eventually built the topic into the number-one issue in America—for a relatively few weeks, at least.

Lesser degrees of exposure among smaller audiences—stockbrokers, for example, or insurance agents—work in similar ways. A rising level of exposure, almost regardless of the level of events, can build public memory, form consensus, and lead to increased public action. Thus, exposure tends to build trends, and measuring that exposure can give hints as to where you are on the trend line.

This can work within as little as a few months, or it can run over many years. We've already mentioned the decline in coverage of politics in the early 1980s, as the American public became desensitized to political issues, and how, at the same time, there was a rise in coverage of the private sector. Corporations began to be seen as the center of economic activity as well as the source of many forms of social responsibility, from education to health to the arts—areas in which government had been playing the major role.

The key idea is that whatever is exposed moves the public's mind. A Trend Watcher, in making an analysis, will want to

determine the source of coverage, whether it is the result of
events or the media's particular sensitivity to them.

Positive Public Memory

Public memory can be positive, too. Take Ronald Reagan's
"Teflon president" image. How did Reagan, in his middle years
as president, manage to escape public criticism when grounds
for it seemed so obvious, especially on such issues as sanctions
against South Africa, the criminal indictment of his secretary
of labor, conflicts of interest among his top aides, and responsibility for soaring budget deficits? By the mid-1980s, there was
a long-running, positive public memory of Reagan, beginning
with his movie career and running through his presidency. His
image was so good that even editors who disagreed with him
had to give him a break. Recognizing this, they reduced their
criticism—which had been substantial in the early years of his
administration—lest they be viewed by their readers and viewers as denigrating a veritable national institution.

After the 1984 presidential elections, criticism virtually
disappeared. Reagan's personal "media power" became enormous, as every politician well knew, and identification with his
opposition could be a political kiss of death. This is the effect
of a well-established, positive public memory.

In media terms, this situation reflects a kind of star quality
that no other politician since Dwight Eisenhower has been able
to muster. Perhaps not surprisingly, about the only other people
in our society who consistently maintain that Teflon image are
Reagan's former colleagues in the entertainment industry. This
explains how rock musicians and movie stars can jump ef-
fortlessly into public issues—hunger, drug abuse, abortion, Nicaragua, apartheid, and all the rest—then jump right out again,
unscathed.

Editors respect the power of public memory and will often
cling to it as a guide for laying out their news until a stronger
signal intervenes. This was shown in the rapid disappearance
of Reagan's Teflon immunity after the 1986 elections. Almost

within hours of the unexpectedly large Democratic gains in Congress, national media editors substantially hiked their criticism of the administration. This was true, we all remember, because "Irangate" broke almost immediately. In a very few weeks, the Iran-contra scandal became the biggest domestic news story in five years. Much of it entailed criticism of the president. By contrast, in October, just a month before the elections, substantial concerns about the administration's performance at Reykjavik produced less than 1 percent of total national coverage. In other words, the public memory of the popular Reagan held until news editors saw the election returns. That's a hard judgment, but the heavy media response to the Iran-contra affair argues persuasively.

The Teflon effect can also happen to corporations. IBM, for example, is seen as the pacesetter in the computer age. Big Blue, as it is known, has consistently had good press. Even news about a downturn in IBM earnings is presented as much a sign of the computer industry's failure as of IBM's. Several other companies have reached this status: Du Pont (in spite of its association with the much-maligned chemical industry), for example, and Chrysler Corporation, under the leadership of Lee Iacocca. (Interestingly, Iacocca has managed to neatly bridge all three categories, with a Teflon-type image in business, media, and, potentially, politics. Even in 1987, when Chrysler came under public and government scrutiny because of some admittedly questionable practices, Iacocca's Teflon image helped both him and his company emerge relatively unscathed.) All three companies have managed to avoid the negative media coverage suffered by their competitors.

Media Sensitivity

We've already discussed in Chapter Four how treatment by reporters of similar successive events can vary from one week to the next—a phenomenon known as media sensitivity. As we've said, what media choose to report or not report, in the broadest sense, reflects what people are learning about society.

Media sensitivity is simply a measurement of the successive amounts of news on a given subject over time. It is calculated by dividing the number of events over a given period with the volume of coverage of such stories. So, if the subject of liability awards from courts in various parts of the country gets progressively less coverage over time, the media is less sensitive about the subject; reporters and editors assume the public has heard all it wants to on the subject and it becomes a "dog bites man" story.

A purist might cavil that no two events are the same and, therefore, the media are responding strictly to the events themselves; in other words, the most recent liability story didn't get as much play as the last one because it didn't have as big an impact on lives, property, and the law. But Trend Watchers are nothing if not pragmatists. You are looking for the *major* movements, not the nitpicking details. Over time, the differences among events will cancel out and a trend in media sensitivity will appear.

Media sensitivity gives an instant measurement of an issue's immediate importance. This is particularly useful in spotting short-term changes. A banker, for example, might see that bankruptcies are being written about with increasing media sensitivity, while reports of gains in employment are scarcely showing up. It's a simple cause-and-effect relationship: You can't see the advances if people aren't hearing about them.

The easiest way to use media sensitivity is to compare your event lines to changes in media coverage of succeeding similar events. You can, if you want, plot media sensitivity on a graph to show rising and falling coverage of any subject of interest. Figure 8-2, for example, shows media sensitivity to air safety in relation to specific airline crashes. Coverage increases slowly with successive events as the media reflect greater concern over air safety after each incident.

You can then take the analytical process a step further. At this stage, keep in mind two things:

- Every subject competes with every other subject for exposure. In this way, travel habits may be linked to something as distant as organized crime or tax reform.

Figure 8-2 Events vs. coverage of air safety, showing rising media sensitivity, 1985.

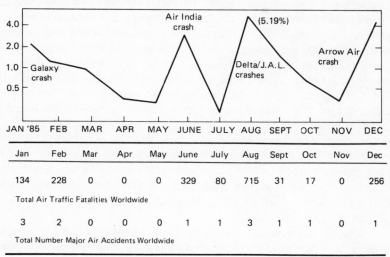

	Jan	Feb	Mar	Apr	May	June	July	Aug	Sept	Oct	Nov	Dec
	134	228	0	0	0	329	80	715	31	17	0	256

Total Air Traffic Fatalities Worldwide

	3	2	0	0	0	1	1	3	1	1	0	1

Total Number Major Air Accidents Worldwide

• It's important to compare apparent noncomparables. This forces you to ask the question "How could an interest in subject *A* be related to a rise or fall in subject *B*?" This helps you make inferences.

Building Constructs and Seeing Countertrends

You will find, as you follow issues of interest, that some of them move in roughly the same direction. It is useful, in fact, to add them together over time to see how they perform collectively. This is, in effect, a means of constructing your own trends by moving to bigger themes and issues, which we call "constructs." It is exactly the opposite of the "micro" approach, which looks for very small, specific movements that relate to narrow business interests. Building constructs is a "macro" approach.

The rise of media attention on corporations in the early 1980s is a good example of a macro perspective. For several years, we counted individual issues: takeovers, bankruptcies, boardroom corruption, insider trading, and a whole series of subjects in which one or more corporations were the central actor. Finally, we saw the light. We lumped them together to get a rough index of how much of the news hole was devoted to all corporate issues, and what kind of a trend this revealed.

Let's go back to an example we've used before. Corporate coverage in the early Reagan years began to rise following the 1984 elections, then really took off. It was only after building a construct of all corporate coverage that we were able to spot a trend in increasing public reliance on the corporate sector as a major source of social action. We were able to determine this because we saw the high priority that corporations were getting in the media and the effect this would ultimately have on the public's mind.

The link between movement of corporate and political coverage represents a classic example of a countertrend. Countertrends appear because news stories must compete. As we described earlier, there is often a direct relationship between the rise of one trend and the decline of another. The link very often relates closely to the way editors see the whole flow of news; they are trying to respond to their audiences. In our example, corporate activity became a partial substitute for political activity, as people looked to the private sector for social action.

When a particular issue declines in coverage, look for whatever is taking its place, even if it is something completely irrelevant. Figure 8-3 shows how corporate coverage displaced political coverage after the 1984 elections. Plotting the corporate construct against the political construct, we begin to see how coverage of the former displaced coverage of the latter. Thus we were able quickly to infer a link: Something the public thought was important—political action—was being replaced by activity of another kind. The public was being led to see corporations in a new light. This has been subsequently substantiated in the experience of many corporations, which have

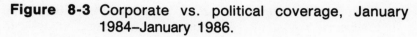

Figure 8-3 Corporate vs. political coverage, January 1984–January 1986.

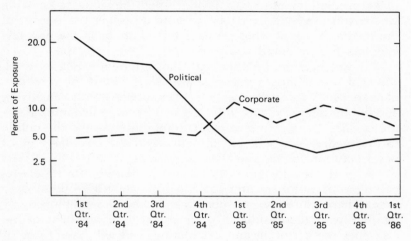

been called upon to take on many social burdens in their communities, and even to assume responsibilities on broader regional and national levels.

Spotting these countertrend movements forces you to make inferences and ask questions that yield the most valuable results—questions you wouldn't otherwise think of and which tell you that something is going on that only a Trend Watcher can spot.

Making Predictions

In Chapter One, we talked about the three principal reasons for watching trends:

1. Making predictions
2. Getting a clear fix on the present and the direction of change currently in progress
3. Following changes in media and their influence

The first reason is clearly the most interesting, but don't jump in too soon. You can't really begin to use trend analysis to make predictions until you have grasped the value of knowing where you are today and of correctly assessing the impact of the media. Much of what we have talked about in the past few chapters has prepared you to do this.

As you become familiar with the numbers, week by week you will note changes that give you clues about the direction of changes. By using the concepts of exposure, media sensitivity, and public memory, your thinking will become dynamic. Bearing in mind the way media react to the public—and the public to the media—you will see the effects of the circular flow of news between media and their audiences.

As you seek to apply these ideas, spend some time eyeballing your numbers and looking for changes in them over time. There is really no substitute for becoming thoroughly familiar with the results of your research. Even if someone else does the counting and calculating, you will have to do at least some of the analysis if you want to obtain the greatest benefit. After you have practiced with your numbers over a period of several months, you likely will have sufficient data to approach the real payoff.

Given these Trend-Watching ideas, and the mechanics of harnessing them discussed so far, how do you actually go about making predictions? We can't emphasize strongly enough that the toughest part is making the *right* preparations—selecting the right publications, properly estimating the news hole, making a solid issues list, and establishing the discipline for a comprehensive monitoring program. Moreover, it is important to test your system. To do this, find an outcome that you can predict. Two obvious candidates are elections or market changes, both of which have quantifiable, immediate results as of a given date. You might, for example, watch the movement of a specific company's stock over a two-month period, during which time you would continually ask yourself the following:

1. What are the things that are likely to affect the stock's price?

2. Irrespective of these answers, how is the stock's price moving?
3. Are there any connections between the two?

It is important that this process be followed carefully. Let the data speak for themselves. Eyeball the data; see what is rising and what is falling with the numbers. Are there issues moving which you wouldn't think are important to the outcome?

By watching the data irrespective of your own subjective expectations, you will set up an alternative and independent set of predictors based on objective data. Then you must link the two. You might find, for example, that there is an intriguing relationship between positive news stories about highway safety and a certain stock's price. Keep your eye on this; it may prove to be a false lead—but, then again, it may not. Such revelations won't necessarily make you a stockbroker, but they can enable you to spot connections that even the insider tip sheets may have missed.

If your Trend-Watching system is working, you should be able to spot some valuable clues. Even if you only see these clues after the fact, you'll know your system is working and you'll be better placed to spot and understand the next major movements.

There is no such thing as making a prediction, then sitting back and reaping its benefits. You'd have to score really big. For those of us with normal amounts of luck, Trend Watching must be an ongoing process. As we've said, in order to postulate a future event, you must first determine where you are and the direction in which you are moving; you must measure from "here" to "there." Otherwise, what appears to be in the future may already be here.

Just as Trend Watching is a continuing process, so is it different from fortune-telling. It's even possible that some of the trends you discover have been around for a number of years, and that you had previously been unaware of them until you examined your data. In other words, Trend Watching isn't necessarily a case of looking into a crystal ball and seeing the world in the year 2022—or even 1992. Trend Watching is seeing movement in today's society that will carry through to tomorrow, whether that "tomorrow" is weeks or years ahead. This is another reason why your initial work with your data will orient you to the present, to begin to see directions of change and to account for particular effects of the media.

There are three ways trends help you predict. Two of them derive from watching continuity—or discontinuity, as the case may be. They emerge from the ongoing process of watching change over time. The third is really a refinement of the discontinuity, but involves adding in the weight of authority of a person or an event. We'll discuss each of these ways.

Extrapolation

The simplest form of prediction is to foresee the extension of a present movement into the future. For example, in the mid-1980s, you can see that an expansion of interest in personal health is virtually unlimited, given widespread concern about diseases like AIDS on the one hand and relative lack of concern about health-care costs on the other. (Examine Figure 8-1 for details on this trend.) You can safely assume that, for the moment, this trend will continue over the short- to medium-term. Your trend line may fluctuate, traveling up, down, or sideways, but odds are that its general path in coming months will follow its earlier course.

There are limits on this kind of prediction, of course. A six-month trend in one direction may only be a one-way swing of a cycle that changes once or twice a year. To rely heavily on extrapolation for more than near-term prediction therefore is risky. Extrapolation is merely the first step in moving from assessing the present to making longer-run predictions. It works because the public's mind changes slowly and is constantly guided in its longer-term action by (1) public memory to previous exposure and (2) media sensitivities that tend to change slowly.

Discontinuities

A more sophisticated approach is to look for sudden and unexpected jerks in continuing trends. All of us tend to expect the status quo—that things will continue from day to day pretty much as is. When they don't, there is more to be known—and perhaps surprises in store, good or bad. When things move suddenly, expect change. This is very much the thinking a stock market chartist uses to spot sudden movements in the price of a particular corporate issue. When he or she sees signs of peaking, or "flags," it is time to expect a change of direction.

A totally unexpected event that takes a lot of attention—the 1986 *Challenger* space shuttle disaster, for example—preempts all other news for several weeks or months. Some of the trends in news reassert themselves in a few weeks. But even these aren't totally irrelevant, because things never return to the status quo afterwards. There is always an effect of heavy exposure. The loss of *Challenger* greatly disturbed America's faith in the future of a wide range of high-technology activities. This faith was a central theme of the early 1980s. Yet there was very little that was not touched by the surge of exposure—over 22 percent of total national coverage for a two-week period. Major events or sudden changes can alter the media map, even in the fine print. It isn't difficult, for example, to foresee the editor of a gardening journal writing about fallout from the Chernobyl disaster—something the editor may never have before considered to be a "local" issue.

In other words, for Trend Watchers, there is no such thing as a false alarm. There's an explanation for every change in media coverage, and it's generally worth the time it takes to figure out what it is. You should always try to explain the blips in your data.

Precursors

Perhaps the finest edge of the trend-analysis art is to spot true smoke signals—the indications of the beginning of a change. These are found less by watching changes in ongoing trends than by learning to see correctly that something is truly new. Needless to say, this requires a certain amount of insight into the present. You can't see what's new without putting it in relief against the old.

Sometimes, this spotting takes a bit of genius. It is the real value of John Naisbitt's work in *Megatrends*—being able to look at massive amounts of grassroots data to spot incipient changes. In essence, Naisbitt is more of a precursor spotter than a Trend Watcher. He not only spotted the movements, but sorted out the ones that seemed to matter.

The precursors Trend Watchers are particularly interested in are those bits of information that can be put together with other data to show some significant shift in direction. They are often associated with authorities—primarily scientists and other researchers—because information from such sources gains immediate credibility and therefore influences society more rapidly. A major event like the *Challenger* disaster is also an "authoritative" change; certainly, it doesn't lack credibility. Most precursors, however, are involved with new ideas that are upstream from current affairs. That's why they are often found in specialized publications. A typical precursor is a one-time signal. It in itself is far more significant than the amount of exposure it gets, either because only a small group of influential people are dealing with it and it is not of broad public interest, or because reporters and editors have yet to gain the insight that the Trend Watcher has already acquired. In other words, the more you watch trends, the better you will become at spotting the mechanics of change and finding the shortcuts.

Here's an example. We learned in early 1986 that the average IQ of women in the armed forces is ten points higher than that of men in the military, and that in this world of "smart" bombs and increasingly sophisticated weapons with no definable combat zone, women are already, in effect, actively involved in combat roles in the U.S. military. Further examination showed that the armed forces were finding that they could use women in increasingly prominent positions; gone were the days when women served merely as auxiliary troops. Inevitably, as more women gain major roles in the military, the situation will project a completely new image about warfare, about the link between soldier and civilian, and, most important, about the ability of women to take over the most macho role of all—the warrior.

Why is this example a smoke signal? It suggests forthcoming changes in many fields:

1. A person in personnel work might consider what implications this information may have for such stereotypical male jobs as mechanics, engineers, and heavy construction workers.
2. A person in a health profession might be interested in looking at the mid- and long-term impact on the health of women who are more physically active, both at work and at play.
3. A person involved in any leisure-time activity might consider revising his or her view of what are traditional women's interests, from gardening to the arts to volunteer work.

As you can see, Trend-Watching numbers have little value without analysis. Indeed, your success as a Trend Watcher will be directly related to two things: the accuracy and thoroughness of your counting and calculating; and the quantity and quality of your analysis. You wouldn't conduct a major market-research program and then merely sit on the numbers. You would scrutinize them for meaning, reading into them a variety of conclusions, each with implications for your business. So, too, with Trend Watching.

Trend Watching, in other words, is a beginning, a point of embarkation from which you can depart to many destinations. To provide maximum value, your Trend-Watching efforts should be disseminated and discussed among appropriate personnel and departments. It is through such efforts that your investment in counting and calculating will begin to pay dividends.

In the next chapter, we will show some graphic representations of Trend-Watching data that may provide further ideas and inspiration.

9
Reaping the Rewards

It's now up to you. You know how the system works. Even more important, you know your business and its need to stay on top of trends. Putting Trend Watching to work is much like the classic definition of a genius—it requires equal parts inspiration and perspiration. There is no substitute for rolling up your sleeves and getting down to it, at whatever level you choose.

Your preparations, your choice of subject matter, the media you pick, and the discipline you establish all determine your success. But Trend Watching does give you something new. You might call it "artificial inspiration." Your reward comes from the new insights that the data provoke, from the questions you are forced to ask, and from the broader horizons you are able to see. Rest assured that your effort will be more than adequately compensated. Even if you never spot an earth-shaking, multimillion-dollar "megatrend," you will still view the world in a new light.

As with so many other things, a picture of a trend is worth a thousand words about it. Trends appear clearest when issues are plotted visually over time. What follows is a series of graphs on ten key sectors of the economy and a number of key issues for which Trend-Watching data have revealed some interesting and useful information in 1984–1987. It's important to note that the time it takes for a book to be produced necessitates our using graphs of trends already passed. Hence, we've had to extrapolate the ends toward which these sets of data *might* have been used. Hypothetical hindsight? Yes. However, the graphs and accompanying analyses in this chapter will, at the very least, get you thinking about the benefits you can derive from your own Trend-Watching data.

The sectors of the economy discussed are:

banking and credit
consumer safety and protection
energy
environment
finance
food and agriculture
health
high-tech
labor
media

Banking and Credit

Figure 9-1 shows four active issues relating to banking and credit for one year, beginning November 1985. Note the rising attention—and, therefore, public concern—during this period about bankruptcies, particularly bank failures. Note also the concern with international economic problems, which excludes trade matters. Also note the persistent decline in concern about inflation. This phenomenon was noted throughout the early 1980s, and in 1986, it reflected the rise in concern over bankruptcies.

What did investors and money managers learn from this information? In this figure are two trends. One is the rising attention in 1986 to international economic problems (other

Figure 9-1 Media coverage of banking and credit issues, November 1985–November 1986.

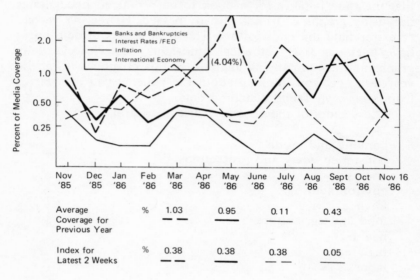

than those that relate directly to the United States, such as foreign trade). Americans were being made increasingly aware that their financial futures depended in part on what happened abroad. In 1987, this became an acute matter, with the decline of the dollar and Japan's overwhelming world economic power. The heavy dotted line reveals a piece of the buildup. The impact of rising foreign competition had been seen for years; the question was, when would it create problems? Its emergence as a major issue in the national media in the mid-1980s clearly foreshadowed that it would remain a concern.

Were you to have foreseen this, you would have been well advised to spread investments over a global scale: to buy in rising economies, for example, such as those of Britain or France, which had currencies relatively low in comparison to the dollar and had strong trading positions. A more extreme strategy might have been to get involved with some of the emerging Third World nations, such as Korea or Brazil.

The second trend evident in Figure 9-1 is the persistent lack of interest in inflation, another trend that has lasted throughout the 1980s. The importance of the deflationary trend has generally been underestimated. What this suggests is that America itself may be a good place to invest—which, of course, is contrary to the trend just mentioned. But a good investor doesn't always go with the flow.

If you were a corporate money manager, these graphs would have been valuable additional tools in helping you determine where to place your stash—in dollars, yen, cruzeiros, or whatever. These are difficult decisions at best, but trend data can give you an edge.

Consumer Safety and Protection

Figure 9-2 plots data beginning in February 1986 and covers one full year. Media coverage of two major consumer issues—transportation safety and food and drug safety—are tracked. Also tracked is media coverage of air safety (a subset of transportation safety) and overall media coverage of consumer safety issues. Immediately noticeable is that transportation safety was the critical issue in determining overall coverage. You can see how the trend line representing all consumer safety issues moves in tandem with transportation safety coverage. But the real news here was that interest in food and drug safety declined. In recent years, consumer issues have been dominated by accidental events involved in transportation safety: air and rail accidents and, to a lesser extent, automobile and truck safety. This is one of the contributing reasons why the federal government has managed to relax restrictions on approving new drugs with virtually no public outcry.

All of this simply tells you that a benign regulatory atmosphere was steadily improving from the producers' point of view. This was true throughout the early 1980s. Short of a

Figure 9-2 Media coverage of consumer safety issues, February 1986–February 1987.

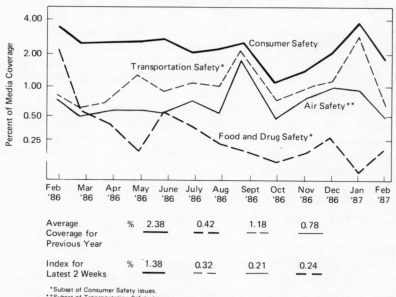

*Subset of Consumer Safety issues.
**Subset of Transportation Safety issues.

Tylenol-type scare, national media did not focus on consumer-product problems to any significant degree during the first half of the decade—which, of course, represents the first Reagan administration. Moreover, there is no sign in these data that this situation is going to change. A pharmaceutical manufacturer might have taken note, pushing ahead a product's development and eventual government approval while the media were looking elsewhere.

On the other hand, the slight rise in both air and transportation safety coverage could have constituted a warning for anyone in those businesses, and they could have been more prepared for a return to regulation and to increased media sensitivity—and, therefore, to consumer concern. A manager of a travel agency could have gained additional business by routing clients away from areas with crowded skies and packed airports.

Energy

Figure 9-3 plots media coverage of U.S. energy issues against coverage of the Chernobyl disaster, oil and gas prices, and nuclear power in the United States. Coverage of energy issues declined persistently through 1986, even though there were major news events. Chernobyl, which occurred in the late spring, raised general concern for a few months over nuclear power in the United States, but by the year's end, coverage of that issue had returned to the previous year's level. Oil and gas prices went into a sharp decline at about the same time. The up-and-down pattern of this price coverage reflects major price movements. Nevertheless, the overall trend was downward, reflecting declining concern over energy supplies. What is significant here is the picture of total coverage, which shows declining concern about energy over the course of the year.

A good stock market investor knows how to go against the trend. As national attention moved away from energy issues, energy stocks moved up less rapidly than the rest of the market and, therefore, were relatively cheap in terms of price-earnings ratios. A reversal of this media trend might bring a return to the psychology of energy scarcity similar to what existed in the 1970s. This is the controlling public memory. Even in 1986, the public hadn't yet gotten used to the idea that oil would ever again be in abundance. There hadn't been much media exposure of the oil surplus, so when oil prices began to rise in the winter of 1987, oil stocks rose also.

Some might contend that you don't need Trend Watching to determine that rising oil costs raise prices of oil stock issues. But knowing the media trends helps greatly with timing— specifically, in knowing how long public attitude toward scarcity or oversupply is likely to last.

Trend data on energy prices is of value to a variety of businesses: building owners, who must keep their properties

Figure 9-3 Media coverage of energy issues, compared with Chernobyl disaster and oil and gas prices, 1986.

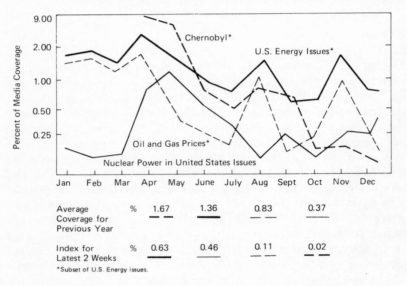

heated and cooled; those in the travel and leisure industries, who know that high energy prices encourage home-based recreation; manufacturers, who depend on energy as an input in their production process; and anyone in the automobile industry.

Environment

Figure 9-4 is a three-year graph covering 1984–86 and portraying media coverage of environmental issues, including air quality, water quality and supply, and other contamination issues. During the early 1980s, the environment maintained a consistent 2 percent level of national media coverage. A significant decline in coverage can be traced during this three-year period. The decline is linked to reduced concern over contamination and

Figure 9-4 Media coverage of environmental issues, January 1984–January 1987.

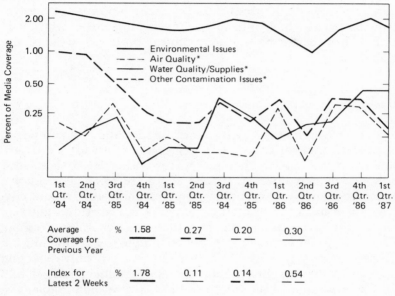

		1st Qtr. '84	2nd Qtr. '84	3rd Qtr. '85	4th Qtr. '84	1st Qtr. '85	2nd Qtr. '85	3rd Qtr. '84	4th Qtr. '85	1st Qtr. '86	2nd Qtr. '86	3rd Qtr. '86	4th Qtr. '86	1st Qtr. '87

Average Coverage for Previous Year % 1.58 0.27 0.20 0.30

Index for Latest 2 Weeks % 1.78 0.11 0.14 0.54

*Subset of Environmental Issues.

a lower number of contamination events reported. But note how the shape of the trend line responds to coverage of air and water quality issues, the dominant environmental concerns.

One key smoke signal in this example is that water was a growing issue. Taken together with precursor information from scientific and community media, it becomes evident that there was strong pressure behind this trend and that the slight rise in the national media coverage was a response to some very strong movements upstream.

If you were in corporate life, this chart would have been good news. It indicates that the media were not responding to contamination events—for example, derailed tank cars and chemical leaks—to the degree that they had in the past. (There were actually fewer events during this period, but this, too, was good news; it meant that the public was less sensitized to these industrial issues.) On the other hand, the concern over water quality—both ground and surface water—was clearly growing. It had high impact on any manufacturer who deals with liquid wastes or any agricultural producer west of the Mississippi.

Finance

Figure 9-5 deals with major financial issues and is a composite of several independently acting factors, none of which are subsets of the others. They are portrayed here to give an idea of how they may interact. Indeed, there are some connections. Note the trend line for money worries, indicating media coverage of availability of credit, including concern over interest rates. This rose slightly after mid-1986 and generally foreshadowed an economic slowdown. But also note the decline during the year in concern over the federal budget, probably reflecting passage of the Gramm-Rudman-Hollings balanced-budget bill. This action reduced the total level of focus on public financial issues, especially after passage of the tax reform bill in midyear. On the other hand, rising throughout the period was an increasing focus on insider trading, which began to dominate the financial pages. The effect? A sharp shift in focus from public to private financing.

There are several signals here. Perhaps most evident was the willingness of the media to relax coverage—and, therefore, to relieve pressure on Congress to lower the budget deficit—following the passage of Gramm-Rudman-Hollings. This meant that problems with the dollar abroad were likely to continue, owing to the need to borrow abroad to meet the deficit.

Also significant was the substantial and consistent rise in coverage of insider trading, anticipating the scandals in the latter part of the year. This coverage led directly to tighter federal regulation of the securities markets. It gave investors some assurance that the worst evils of 1929 won't be repeated.

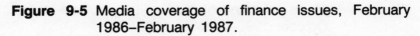

Figure 9-5 Media coverage of finance issues, February 1986–February 1987.

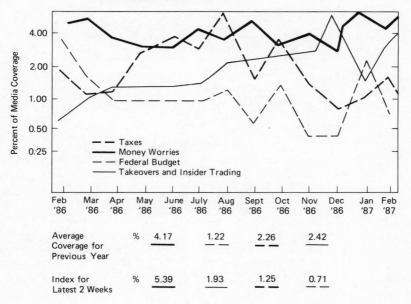

On the other hand, others might have seen it as a telltale of the end of the stockmarket boom if regulators, backed by Congress, decided to tighten rules governing takeovers, thus evaporating one of the principal forces that had been pushing up stock prices.

Food and Agriculture

Figure 9-6 shows media coverage of food and agriculture issues from October 1985 to October 1986—harvest to harvest. Note the spike in late winter, as agricultural stories reflected the personal suffering of farmers and their families during bleak times, a regular seasonal feature of coverage during the mid-

Figure 9-6 Media coverage of food and agriculture issues, October 1985–October 1986.

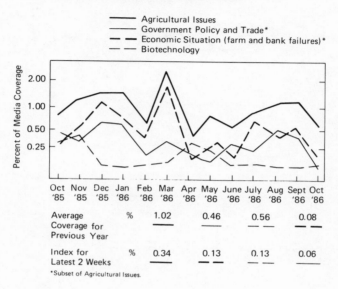

Average Coverage for Previous Year	%	1.02	0.46	0.56	0.08
Index for Latest 2 Weeks	%	0.34	0.13	0.13	0.06

*Subset of Agricultural Issues.

1980s. This notwithstanding, there was a slight decline throughout the year in stories about government remedies to help the farm situation in general.

This graph was bad news for those in agriculture. It shows declining public concern with agricultural issues in general, and little demand for government remedies to ease farmers' plight. What it suggests is that the public had begun to live with "the farm problem" in the same fashion that it "lives" with the problems of the homeless and the needy. If you were in the food business—a grocer, distributor, or restaurateur, for example—this information would have foretold both good and bad: On one hand, prices were likely to drop or remain low; on the other hand, sources of key commodities might have become unstable as some farmers were driven out of business. One solid plus on the supply side is that as traditional products like grain and milk would become less attractive, farmers would be "encouraged" to produce more exotic vegetables and fruits, making these more widely available and lowering the price.

Health

Figure 9-7 reflects the most heavily exposed topic in the issues list, and a consistently growing one. As the graph for 1986 shows, the driving force in coverage of health issues is the rise in concern over AIDS. The media have paralleled this concern with a consistent attempt to portray medical advances in a favorable light. Of particular significance is the jump, in the fall of 1986, in concern over medical costs, as the vast impact of caring for AIDS patients began to be recognized. This jump represented a major shift in attitudes toward health issues in the 1980s, reflecting for the first time how as much attention was being paid to health care *costs* as to health care *quality*.

What Figure 9-7 tells us is that rising concern with health costs turned upward sharply for the first time in years when associated with AIDS. The nation began to understand what it must pay for good health. Employers would have expected some of this "understanding" to show up in negotiating benefits packages: As costs increase, the amount and types of coverage would come under closer scrutiny. On the other hand, this trend presaged strong public pressure to hasten medical advances—to approve drugs and devices sooner, for example—to deal with the AIDS menace. One might have also assumed that the eased regulation would have an effect on other drug and device manufacturers. One result could be an ever-booming health-services marketplace, with businesses and industries springing up at record rates.

One other aspect of the data is that as concern with AIDS grew, there was no diminishing pressure to find answers to cancer and other prevalent killers. This means that the boom in the medical business would not be confined simply to AIDS.

Figure 9-7 Media coverage of health issues, January 1986–January 1987.

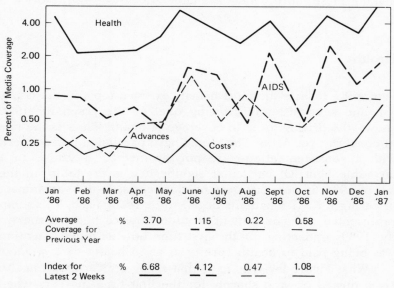

*Includes Medicare/Medicaid and Health Insurance Issues.

High-Tech

Figure 9-8 reflects people's concern about high-tech issues in 1986. Much of the time, the media's high-tech beat was spent reacting to the collapse of expectations for America's space program following the *Challenger* disaster. Other high-tech coverage was generally depressed all year, even extending to the media's penchant to extol the virtues of advances in computer technology. Also note that concern with competition from foreign high-tech suppliers did not emerge as a significant issue in 1986; it would take off in 1987, under business and political pressure.

For this particular year, the trends in this area were somewhat misleading. Obviously, the long-term view of Americans

Figure 9-8 Media coverage of high-tech issues, January 1986–January 1987.

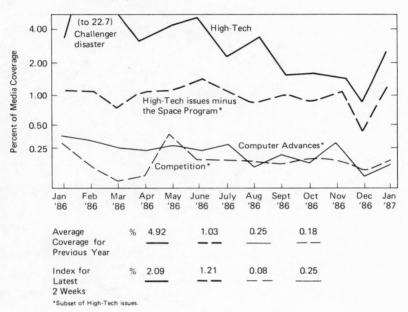

is that high-tech will "fix" anything. Therefore, this figure should be read as a measure of the reversal in the long-term trend, and the sudden upward shift at the end should be looked at as a signal of a reversion to the norm. As for 1986, it was mostly a case of "a few bad apples"—*Challenger* and Chernobyl, for example—spoiling the entire technological barrel. By early 1987, the media began to enthuse over high-tech: new and better computers, superconductive materials, and biogenetic achievements.

An educator looking at this graph might have supposed that doubts about science that appeared after the *Challenger* accident could easily be dispelled and that it would be possible to attract students back into astrophysics and related sciences. Small manufacturers of high-tech products might have seen it

Figure 9-9 Media coverage of labor issues, December 1985–
December 1986.

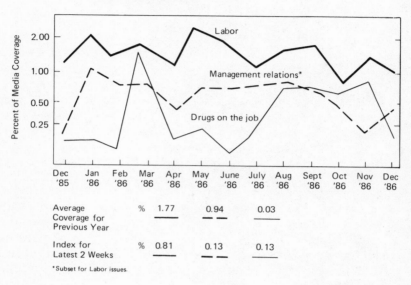

as an encouraging sign for raising research-and-development
funds or accelerating development of a new product.

Labor

Figure 9-9 shows how, in 1986, labor issues were essentially
steady, with a slight declining trend reflecting relative industrial
peace and a declining focus on unions as a power center. Note
that the question of drugs in the workplace, not counted as a
subset of the labor issues trend, received almost as much
coverage as did the topic of management relations.

This situation is in keeping with a general trend to turn
coverage of the workplace toward actual productivity problems
and away from traditional labor-management issues. This in-

cludes more focus on such problems as employee ownership, workers' rights, and new forms of employee associations which include middle management; and less focus on the wage package. The proliferation of these issues strongly suggested that a whole new labor debate was on its way, with both parties looking to new forms of employee-employer relationships and union reform. Human resource managers might have anticipated that employees would use increased productivity as a principal argument to gain higher wages. Managers could have foreseen a need to be more sensitive to issues that affect workers personally, including their safety and privacy.

Media

Figure 9-10 shows media coverage of its own industry, with subset trends showing coverage of management changes and takeovers and criticism. In the early 1980s, the major media were forced to respond to heavy criticism for alleged abuses of its political powers and biases. They responded by increasingly reporting about—literally covering—themselves. As the three-year graph shows, the media first shied away from reporting criticism of their own activities during 1985, but were forced to reexamine themselves—albeit briefly—during the Iran-contra affair. But this phenomenon was short-lived, and the media were not put on the defensive again. A more significant media trend was the impact of ownership. This, too, can affect media content, as reflected in fears that General Electric's traditional conservatism might affect NBC, which it purchased in 1986, or that foreign ownership of the media (Rupert Murdoch, United Press International) might significantly alter the character of media coverage.

This graph is particularly interesting as a precursor to the events of 1987, when the media were again forced to defend themselves for their heavy coverage of the Iran-contra affair, as well as their tactics in covering certain presidential candidates. The issue here was raw media power. In 1986, it looked as though the media had dealt with the conservative criticism

Figure 9-10 Media coverage of its own industry, January 1985–April 1987.

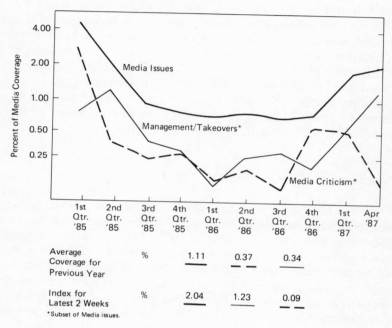

of the 1980s, but the rising trend line in early 1987 shows that this issue was not simply a matter of satisfying one part of the political spectrum.

Media-relations types would have been well advised to look very carefully at the concerns of media management: how they are dealing with advertisers, how they instruct their news editors, for example. The media business had a great deal at stake in this debate and may very well have concluded that it had more in common with other corporate entities than it had ever acknowledged before. In other words, it might well have been right for business to talk to media as a business.

What's not seen in this figure is how the sharp rise in the media's criticism of themselves was almost completely parallel to a strong revival of political coverage. Until the Iran-contra affair, political coverage had not regained the robust strength it had during the 1970s. But in the fall of 1986 that changed. The media immediately began to ask questions about its own role in American government. You would not have been surprised that, a few months later, the media not only had the power to smash presidential candidate Gary Hart, but that they would spend significant additional time and space deciding it was right to do so. What we see in this figure is the beginning of a great constitutional debate over the role of the Fourth Estate, an issue that extends to the rights of every American.

Focusing In

Graphics also can be useful when focusing on smaller issues. Here are several examples of specific trend lines, as reported in *Issues Management Letter* during 1986 and 1987, along with some comments about the significance of those trends at the time. It will give you some insight into how you can interpret the data's importance.

Terrorism: Domestic versus International (1/12/86)

The number of domestic incidents of terrorism had been very small, compared to such actions abroad. Figure 9-11 shows how media coverage focused most heavily on incidents like the *Achille Lauro* affair and several airport bombings. By comparison, coverage of domestic terrorism had been small but was rising. The key point is that because of major international events, the media became increasingly sensitized to minor incidents in this country.

Corporate Governance (4/20/86)

Figure 9-12 is a simple graph showing a continuing interest in corporate governance, with a slight downtrend over the six-

Figure 9-11 Media coverage of terrorism—domestic vs. international, August 1985–January 1986.

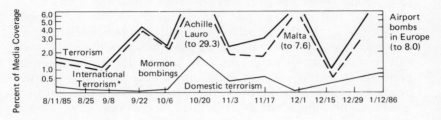

*Subset of terrorism issues.
Note: Media coverage was tracked in two-week periods.

Figure 9-12 Media coverage of corporate governance, November 1985–April 1986.

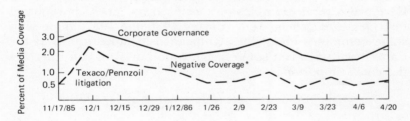

*Subset of Corporate Governance issues.
Note: Media coverage was tracked in two-week periods.

month period shown. Coverage of the Texaco-Pennzoil litigation closely paralleled the overall movement, making it the dominant issue in this category. Clearly, the Texaco-Pennzoil issue was shaping this entire group of topics in this period.

Ethics in Government (5/4/86)

Figure 9-13 shows a sharp rise in media attention paid to ethics-in-government questions, prompted largely by issues in

Figure 9-13 Media coverage of ethics in government, December 1985–May 1986.

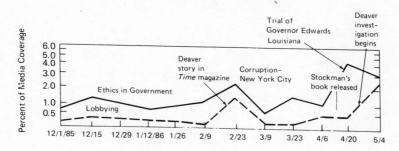

state and local politics. But note the rising concern over ethics in the federal government, beginning with the first articles on the Michael Deaver conflict-of-interest affair. This was one of the issues that eventually led to sharper criticism of the Reagan administration later in the year.

Health and Environment (7/2/86)

Figure 9-14 contrasts the steady rise in health issues, which began even before the AIDS scare, with a decline in environmental coverage between 1984 and early 1986. These issues are often linked, since environmental issues frequently involve cancer and other specific health issues. The environmental issues line, incidentally, did not include industrial accidents such as the one in Bhopal, India. But had they been included, the trend would have remained essentially the same, except for a sharp spike in late 1984–early 1985, followed by a resumed decline.

Network Coverage of Liberal Issues (8/24/86)

Figure 9-15 shows the portion of evening network news broadcasts devoted to several liberal issues for a six-month

Figure 9-14 Media coverage of health and environment issues, 1984–mid-1986.

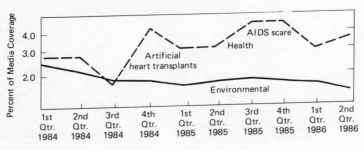

Figure 9-15 Network coverage of liberal issues, March–August, 1986.

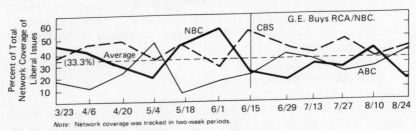

period: social equity, environment, arms control, and others. Note that in the period prior to its merger with General Electric, NBC was below the average for the three networks only twice. Following the merger, NBC's coverage of liberal issues consistently remained below the average. CBS stayed as the most liberal network; ABC was relatively conservative, but less so as NBC shifted.

Futures Issues (10/22/86)

Figure 9-16 represents a construct—an attempt to build a new issue we haven't tracked before out of other data on the

Figure 9-16 Futures construct of media's coverage of four major issues vs. high-tech issue, January 1984–October 1986.

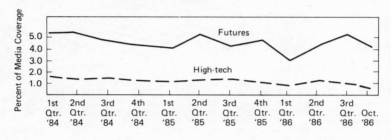

Note: Futures trend line incorporates media coverage of education, environment, immigration, and high-tech (not including Shuttle program) issues.

issues list. The solid line represents an amalgam of four categories: education, environment, immigration, and high-tech. These combined issues offer a prospective look at society; a second line represents a subset for high-tech alone. Over the two-and-a-half-year period of coverage shown in the figure, there was a clear decline in both segments, suggesting less optimism with or concern for future change.

Criticism of Reagan and his Administration (10/11/86)

In Figure 9-17, all the lines described a shallow valley, as criticism of all aspects of the Reagan administration declined through 1984, remained low throughout 1985 and early 1986, only to rise in the final quarter of that year following news of the Iran-contra affair. Note that trends showing criticism of the president and his administration, though at times seeming to move in opposite directions, in the long run moved in the same way. It is significant that the media generally refrained from criticism during the period of Reagan's greatest popularity.

Religious and Moral Issues (12/17/86)

Over the previous two years, there had been a gradual rise in religious issues. Figure 9-18 shows that this trend was almost

Figure 9-17 Media criticism of Reagan administration, January 1984–November 1986.

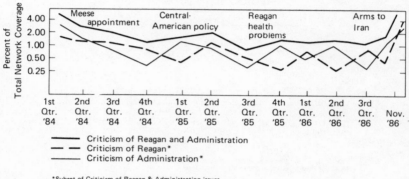

Figure 9-17 Media criticism of Reagan administration, January 1984–November 1986.

doubling, with a concurrent increase in coverage of social morality questions such as pornography and obscenity. Abortion coverage, on the other hand, clearly declined, indicating a shift in attitude away from this conservative standby issue to a new, broader social ethic.

Figure 9-18 Media coverage of religious, moral, and abortion issues, 1985–1986.

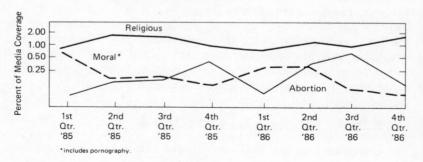

Figure 9-18 Media coverage of religious, moral, and abortion issues, 1985–1986.

Figure 9-19 Positive vs. negative economic news, 1986.

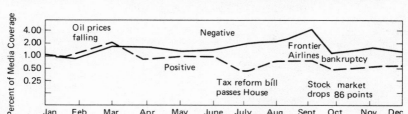

Positive vs. Negative Economic News (1/15/87)

During the year 1986, negative economic news rose considerably, as shown in Figure 9-19. Positive news, on the other hand, rose with falling oil prices, but then declined for the rest of the year, even after tax reform was passed. Note the peak in negative news in September, just before the stock market dropped 86 points. This was clearly foreshadowed by movements in the National Media Index on these issues. But at the time, Wall Street watchers ascribed it to computer trading. Only in March 1987 did the Securities and Exchange Commission conclude that, based on its own research, negative economic news was the cause of the precipitous drop.

Corporate vs. Political Issues (1/29/87)

Figure 9-20 looks at all corporate issues (including governance, shown in Figure 9-12). This graph shows a rise during 1986 from the previous year. Significantly, coverage of politics also rose during this period and, contrary to what might have been expected during earlier patterns, the focus on the corporate sector did not decline. In other words, the two sectors of media interest became complementary instead of contrasting. This was the first smoke signal foretelling trouble for the image

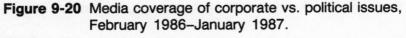

Figure 9-20 Media coverage of corporate vs. political issues,
February 1986–January 1987.

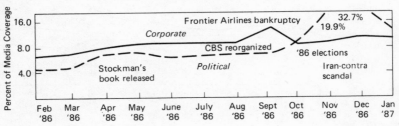

of the private sector, about which pundits and academicians began to write several months later.

The figures in this chapter give you a fast look at some recent history involving the national media. They will convey an idea of the macrotrends affecting American life just as this book is going to press. You may wish to use them—or your own versions based on them—in devising your own scheme. However, remember that these trends are about broad events beyond the battle you are probably fighting in your business. As we have shown with issues lists and other examples, to make Trend Watching work for you, you must get down to specifics. It's no good knowing the megatrends—the major movements in society—if you can't relate them to your daily life.

On the other hand, you must be able to relate the macro-trends to the microtrends. What we have shown here is an introduction to the former, with the hope that you can better focus on the latter to meet your own objectives.

10

Why Trend Watching Works: Some Theory

Trend Watching can be only as good as the ideas behind it. If the ideas aren't current, the system isn't worth using. And the ideas behind your Trend-Watching system grow out of up-to-date thinking about information.

What follows is, admittedly, complex. For this grounding in Trend-Watching basics, we must examine some still-evolving theories of information, the scientific process of communication, how information flows move society, and how all of this relates to the ability to make predictions. The basic idea is that understanding the force of information on society helps Trend Watchers determine in what direction it is moving.

You needn't read this chapter to be a Trend Watcher, but we advise you to do so. Your success as a Trend Watcher is directly linked to your ability to understand the nature and power of information. The theory is an important part of the Trend-Watching process.

The Uncertain Future

It is characteristic of an era of uncertainty, such as our present time, that many risks and challenges are less than clear-cut. Even more difficult is the fact that the strategies for dealing with these uncertainties are only beginning to evolve. This makes Trend Watching doubly valuable: It allows you to stay ahead of the pack while the pack becomes increasingly confused about where it is going.

Too often, the future is made to look scary by "experts" posing as leaders, who feed on this uncertainty. To be sure, there is a legitimate function in warning of such perils as ravaging disease, environmental dangers, or radical economic swings. But all too often, with the scare comes a portrayal of the future in terms people can't comprehend and will instinctively reject. People don't *want* to live intimidated by sterile housing, for example, or work with temperamental computers, or be served by robots who know more than they do. The "inevitable future" posed by some futurists too often seems to exclude people, as far as who they are now and what they are doing today.

This scariness and uncertainty is typical of a new era. The present era, the information age, is one most notably marked by massive changes in the quantity and quality of information available to us. The anxiety of this era is exacerbated by the view, common in Western thought for most of the past two centuries, that nothing is constant, that change will accelerate, that only the best and brightest will be able to cope. What we must understand is that there is more opportunity in these changes—at the human level—than there is risk or fear.

The most important point here is that the driving force of this era—information—must ultimately move through *people*. This is an age of human-based information, not energy-based materials. This point is all too often ignored by futurists, who are only now finding out that the most important value added in robotic manufacturing comes from the skills, experience, and training of the people attending them, or that the value of information-intensive software well exceeds that of the physical hardware that drives it. We are also recognizing that artificial intelligence will not be permitted to do our social thinking for us. *People* will inevitably seek and retain control. We will largely determine our own pace of change. If we don't want C3PO, HAL, Robocops, or other high-tech, humanoid beasts for buddies, servants, and masters, these products will fail in the marketplace, where human beings make the choices.

But fear of the future will persist, no matter how high the tech. Because we're at a historical threshhold, moving into a new age, it's often easier for futurists—and business people— to be scared than to be sensible. Sensationalism sells newspapers, airtime, products, and services. But for most of us, fear of the future is irrational, denying the professional vision we all need. As changes persist, that vision becomes as important to have as it is difficult to acquire.

Invariably, the further back we look, the further forward we can see. Where history moves in longer cycles—as in population changes, weather cycles, or such long-term economic cycles as the Kondratieff wave—a broader view is needed. These are all useful tools that depend on our reaching into the past to see ahead and meshing that with trend analysis. Trends project a picture of the future, step by step. There is no great jump, no quantum leap—just a smooth glide, whose direction will be true if you have looked at all the right data and set your sails accordingly.

It's fair to ask why Trend Watching is particularly appropriate now. There are two reasons:

- The need to make sense of daily inflows of information becomes more acute as more data pour in.
- The advances of the information age, as we'll soon explain, give us the tools to meet that need.

Dawn of a New Era

Much as energy was used before the advent of the Industrial Revolution, so were people using information well ahead of the information age. People used information values unconsciously, in an age when value was created chiefly through the power to move and change the material world—to turn steel into cars, for example; or soil, seeds, and water into a cornucopia of food. From actuaries to advertisers, xerographers to zoologists, the information industry (often lumped into the economy's vast "service sector") today encompasses a steadily increasing portion of the nation's wealth. Marc Porat, then a Stanford University doctoral student, estimated in 1967 that just under half of the value of the American economy was generated by expenditures on information. Consider how many computers and copiers have been built in the two decades since.

The information age is a reflection of this growth—the elevation of "information" to a level of basic value on a par with "matter" and "energy." It requires a new description of our day-to-day universe. In human history, changes from one age to another come only with a reassessment of values and outlook. It is this kind of momentous shift in values that validates the perennial Boy Scout wisdom. For years, purveyors of everything from computers to college courses to consultants on every imaginable subject have sounded the warning: "Be prepared."

Simplistic advice, perhaps, but true. The successful entrepreneur of the information age is the person who knows how to make the best use of the modern tools designed to obtain, process, and manipulate data: the computers, copiers, satellites, fiberoptics, and a myriad other technologies on hand or on the horizon. Obviously, great rewards will go to the creators of such tools, and to those who service them and teach their use. These will be the public utilities of tomorrow—the information companies that will increasingly become the "power" companies—the utilities—of the information age.

But the similarities between information companies and electric utilities end there. Information is not like energy. There are infinite varieties of it, and it won't run out; indeed, information will proliferate. Moreover, the value of any piece of information will, for the near future at least, be based on a largely subjective appraisal. The economics of information is still in its embryonic stages. Yet there is little argument that information is power and that, increasingly, the key to business profits—and, some would say, survival—is knowing how to find information, acquire it, make use of it, sell it, or otherwise profit from it. In the coming years, an unprecedented amount of our society's research-and-development dollars will go toward these activities.

It will not be a smooth transition. For the foreseeable future, the information age will involve using information to improve the things people do based on values set in the mid- to late-twentieth century. There will be no "pure" economic system based solely on information. For one thing, it isn't possible to have information without energy, and neither information nor energy is of much use without industrial materials. Increasingly, though, people will need less energy and fewer materials and more information.

The Value of Information

Information has value only when it is used. In its pristine, uncommunicated state, information is like a lump of coal underground; its value is created only when it is refined and consumed. But, unlike coal, information is not destroyed by consumption. Information obeys many of the physical laws that apply to energy, but with one great difference: There is no lack of supply.

The complexities of the demand for information make it even more difficult to establish its value. To be certain about the value of any one piece of data, it is necessary to know a good part of the story in the first place. Consider the question, "Where are the jewels buried?" The answer is valuable only if you already know that (1) there are jewels, (2) they are buried somewhere, and (3) if you find them, they're yours. Ultimately, the answer to the question is the only one that has value.

In any age, there are great rewards in finding key pieces to an endless number of puzzles: Should we launch the new product line? Expand the division? Buy in? Sell out? Once the initial premises of such questions are known, whole crews of investigators, armed with the latest techniques, can be marshaled to ferret out the remaining valuable clues. Asking the right questions is the key.

Of course, valuable clues don't exist by themselves. Their value is always tied to other bits of information, and the assessment of any one piece of information is usually subjective. There is always room in the information age for those entrepreneurs who have a good gut-level sense of these values. But success is inextricably linked to the ability to keep that information closely held, so as to be able to act on it. If it's not secret, the value of the information will quickly wither.

Thus, there are two critical aspects of the value of information you must be aware of to be able to act ahead of the pack: establishing relationships among bits of information, and keeping the knowledge to yourself (or at least only among trusted colleagues).

Some Basic Concepts

It took years for Newton's theories to yield the Industrial Revolution. And Einstein's impact is still seen only imperfectly through the efforts of NASA and in scientific laboratories. Why should anyone make the Great Leap Forward to embrace the information age?

To answer this question, you first need to understand one of the fascinating realities of the late twentieth century: that the "energy crisis" and the information age arrived at roughly the same time. This was not mere coincidence. The most recent theories on the behavior of energy have strongly influenced, or have led directly to, the development of a scientific theory of information. That theory was born of necessity. It was plain that matter and energy alone could not begin to explain the physical universe. More important for our purposes, they could not fully explain its value.

Consider the human body. On today's market, the materials that constitute a body are worth perhaps a couple hundred dollars. The body's energy input, based on its daily food intake, is also relatively small compared to the value placed on human life, or even the value placed on the brain-guided work a human being can do. Obviously, there is something beyond mere matter and energy here—a value to explain both the physical existence and the dynamics of biological creation. In this and in many other ways, it has become clear that the world's works cannot be explained entirely in terms of matter and energy. Increasingly, information has become the missing link.

In recent decades, scientists have begun to deal with the problems of information's value: of how much data could be sent over a telephone wire, for example, or the role of "noise" in communications. In the process, scientists have developed crude thinking machines. They quickly found that the new technologies of electronics were instructive, and offered vast new opportunities as well. Jeremy Campbell, in his 1982 book *Grammatical Man*, describes the dawn of the age:

> It was not until the 1940s that information was defined as a scientific term, and this definition was quite new, unlike any in the standard dictionaries. Yet in a curious way, the concept of information, by being defined precisely enough to satisfy mathematicians and telecommunications engineers, became increasingly fascinating to nonscientists. The word began to recapture some of its meanings which had fallen into disuse. The view arose of information as an active agent, something that does not just sit there passively, but "informs" the material world, much as the messages of the genes instruct the machinery of the cell to build an organism, or the signals from a radio transmitter guide the intricate path of a vehicle on its journey through space.

Campbell's explanation of information as an active agent is the one to bear in mind. It is the enormous power of information to alter the elements it "informs" that makes this an information age. Physical scientists think in terms of particles, atoms, and molecules, biologists in terms of organisms. Increasingly, information scientists—electrical engineers, biogeneticists, and computer designers, among others—are thinking in terms of streams of digital pulses furiously transmitting enormous quantities of electronic signals that, when combined, have meaning and value. Some also see information as a social force, with people being the ultimate recipients of the transmitted messages, whether in the form of electronic mail or as chemical reactions that enable the blood to flow unrestricted through the body. The scientific background not only provides authority for the study of information, but it also is a guide to thinking. (For those who want to dig deeper into the scientific background, there is no better source than Jeremy Campbell's very readable work.)

We must not confuse the power of information with its sheer volume. All too often, the information age is seen as a glut—the sudden generation of much more data than people can possibly assimilate and use. But that vast accumulation is the *result* of the new age, not its cause or even its principal characteristic. By focusing on the glut of data you miss the point. The "value" in information refers to that vital last element that creates value in a productive process—that final piece of data that tells where the metaphoric jewels are buried or, more specifically, what product or service the market really needs, what a key production factor will cost, or why it's time to cut your losses.

It should not be surprising that information theory was discovered by an engineer working at Bell Laboratories, the same facility in which the nation's telephone network—the world's greatest communication system—was developed. In 1948, William Shannon published two papers in the *Bell System Technical Journal* on the theory of the transmission of messages from one place to another. At the time, Shannon generalized on the principles he had discovered and postulated laws applicable to all types of information, not merely telephone messages.

William Shannon not only developed what were soon recognized as universal laws about the behavior of information, but he also linked them theoretically to earlier ideas about the behavior of energy. Picking up on the Second Law of Thermodynamics—which states that energy always changes from a concentrated form to a less-concentrated, less-powerful form—Shannon said that information depreciates and becomes more disorderly as it passes from one state to another. Like energy, information loses value as it is transmitted. The message encounters greater levels of noise as it moves. (*Noise*, in this context, refers to information that has no meaning, as opposed to the *message*, which is information that has use and value.) By scientific methods, Shannon showed that the measurements for the behavior of both information and energy were the same.

It is difficult to underestimate the historical importance of Shannon's discoveries. But so fast do matters advance in modern society that within very few years there seemed to be an overreaction. Shannon himself wrote that the theory "had perhaps ballooned to an importance beyond its actual accomplishments." Yet Shannon's work was one of those contributions for which history seemed to be prepared. As has happened with so many of society's key discoveries, other people had been working on the links between energy and information even as Shannon's work appeared in print. One reason was that World War II had forced scientists to think about coding and language problems inherent in the use of radar, which was being employed to track ships and planes. A crucial link to making use of radar's information was identifying a bit of data within the movement of an electron. Once this was established, it became possible for the information age to blossom with more sophisticated uses of energy and with what has become known as "electronics."

The concept of informational noise is a peculiar key to understanding Trend Watching. On one level, separating noise from messages is the kind of problem communications engineers must deal with daily when working with telecommunications lines and networks; the noise is the interference—static, for example—that impairs clear communications. On a broader level, noise also refers to the tendency within society to distort information and, sometimes, to destroy its meaning.

A good example of noise comes from the old parlor game of "Telephone." The game is played as one person creates a message, then passes it around a room via confidential whispers from one person to the next. The last person then announces the message out loud. Inevitably, the message has become distorted over the various person-to-person transmissions, often bearing no relation to the original. At some point during the communications process, the message deteriorates into noise. That's an overly simple example of information depreciation in a social context, yet it applies equally to messages passed through more formal systems. Such noise plays an important role in the media and in the communication of daily news.

Noise is an inevitable product of the times. One of the perils is that scientific advance and the translation of its findings to daily life occur with increasingly shorter lags. Even today, scientists are not in full agreement about the links between energy and information. But people's need to take advantage of every possible shred of information is so great that they feel obliged to put these ideas to use as quickly as possible. That, again, is the characteristic of moving into a new age. The level of uncertainty—noise—is so high that people must take steps to overcome it. The risk of failure is only more noise and more uncertainty. In business or personal life, that translates into a lack of vision and an inability to plan or, ultimately, to compete. The information glut we referred to earlier is, in reality, largely the reception of data as noise instead of as meaning. What Trend Watching is all about is sorting through the noise and turning it into meaningful messages.

It is fair to ask whether information defined as something flowing over a wire is the same sort of thing as a bit of news about, say, a kickback scandal in the boardroom at company X. For our purposes, it is. Undoubtedly, news about the scandalous management, as it travels from mouth to mouth, suffers a distortion of meaning as happens in the game of "Telephone" or as electronic data suffer when passing along a wire. In all cases, the principle of communication is the same. What started as an allegation of a relatively small scandal may ultimately result in a CEO resignation before the allegation is even proved correct. The CEO was felled, not by the facts, but by the noise.

The Science of Language

The language that communicated the story about company X followed the same rules of behavior that apply to electronic communication. These rules not only tell about the value of information, but they give Trend Watchers their first clues about trend development and the ability to make predictions.

Science offers Trend Watchers a double break: First, it allows you to make sure your methods are as up to date as the new age itself; second, it shows the way to cope with that age. Modern discoveries in language help Trend Watchers observe and even predict information flows.

Let's begin with simple two-way communication. Two people cannot communicate unless each has a base of knowledge about what the other is going to say. That base of knowledge must contain two elements. First, both speaker and receiver must have some set of common ideas regarding the things about which they're talking, whether it be new potatoes or nuclear physics. More important, they must use and understand the same code of communications—what we call a language. Within that language, both must understand what things are called or how to express ideas.

These features ensure the reliable, creative process we call communication. Both kinds of knowledge—what things are and how to talk about them—are part of the code, or language, of communication. They allow for the knowledgeable to speak to the ignorant, with some assurance of success. In communication, both sides know the basic code, but not all its messages. For example, if one side doesn't know the meaning of the word *french fries*, the other party can use other words like *potatoes*, *deep-fried*, and so on to further describe the subject. This toolbox of ideas is part of the system of language.

For many years, linguists were seen by society as odd people who spent their lives on the Latin genetive, or who translated poetry from an obscure language. Things have changed a bit. Today, linguists stand at the forefront of modern thinking. The information age has created a whole new range of needs that linguists can fulfill—in support of psychiatry, education, and our understanding of thought, among other fields. In more practical terms, new or newly discovered languages drive many different types of communications systems, from genetic codes to computer languages to interplanetary signals.

The process of coding began with the development of telegraph and radio signals. Those first methods of translating messages into discrete "dits" and "dahs" (in the case of the telegraph) were among the first formalized communication codes outside the verbal activity we call speech. Coding now has a variety of uses, from governing communications among computers and other electronic devices to probing signals by which messages are gained from waves bounced back to the sender, as in radar. Most strikingly, these same coding processes are found in nature—in biological transmissions via genetic coding between generations or to various parts of the body. In fact, the revolution now under way in genetic engineering is very much a product of new knowledge about languages. Breaking down the genetic code was the key to finding how genes control the body, make us vulnerable or invulnerable to disease, and determine growth and development.

Codes are vital. They allow us to carry out two seemingly contradictory functions at the same time: that communication be at once reliable and unpredictable. But these actually are complementary actions, ensuring that a message both gets across and also contains valuable bits of information. To communicate effectively, there must be a high probability that the message will be understood—that, for example, the other party will have some idea of what you're talking about when you mention "french fries." Understanding is assured when both sides know the basic code.

But codes alone do not successful communication make. If the receiver knows in advance everything that is being transmitted, there will be no value in the message. It's like asking a waiter "How's the soup today?" You know how he'll answer. The exchange is more one of etiquette than a request for data. If there is total predictability of the answer, there will be no value to the communication. So, the paradox of effective communication is that it must be both reliable and unpredictable. If the waiter responds, "The soup tastes like dishwater today," that would be considerably more meaningful than the predictable, "It's quite good." Indeed, it would be news.

The problem of combining the right amounts of reliability and unpredictability is the task of language specialists, the professional experts in coding. Being able to spot the unpredictable with a significant level of reliability is the key task of Trend Watchers.

English is a particularly rich and flexible language. Used by professionals around the world, it has become the code of modern international business. Even its odd spelling nuances offer assurance of communication. When you see a misspelling, you may or may not spot it immediately because there is usually sufficient material around the misspelled word so that the context is preserved and no meaning is lost. (The word *rithem* might not mean much, but in the sentence, "That song has a great rithem," the additional information gives meaning to a mangled spelling.) This feature of ensured meaning is one of the ways language increases the chances of a message being communicated successfully.

Probability is achieved by offering these forms of repetitive signals or built-in backups, which ensure that meaning is conveyed. A great deal of redundancy is needed in sending signals to an interplanetary space platform to assure that no communication is lost. In daily conversation, there is room for more improbability because the risk of a misstatement generally does not involve a great loss of effort. Moreover, people commonly take time to restate their words or explain their thoughts; facial expressions, hand gestures, and body language help, too. Not being programmed in advance, like a missile communications system, people have flexibility in their speech, with the result that discourse can be more creative. Hence, there is the possibility for fiction, lyrics, and poetry.

We take this creativity for granted, of course. In a world confined largely to speech, coding systems don't appear to be very important. We converse so naturally and have so many nonverbal ways of providing redundancy that it is second nature to communicate in these multiple ways. But in the information-age world of electronic communications, the balance between probability and improbability is more difficult to maintain.

Being able to design and read codes is the hallmark of people in the information age. Just a few years after Bell Lab's William Shannon published his first papers on information theory, another dramatic discovery came along: DNA, or deoxyribonucleic acid, the genetic building block of life. Since that time, a whole new biological world has emerged, one not even imagined a generation ago. Simultaneously, computers and electronic communications networks were beginning to enter the commercial marketplace. All of these events called for new skills in reading codes and understanding communication. Although each development required a different approach, the basic principles of coding and communication remained the same throughout.

Findings on the study of genetic communication are at the heart of the biogenetic revolution just beginning to change people's lives. The information age and its discoveries are putting biology at the top of the sciences. By adding a value for information to that for energy and matter, researchers will at last find an explanation for why human beings are worth so little in material terms when we know them to be so valuable. Thanks to genetics, we know that it is the information base and the system used to create and sustain human beings that must be termed priceless by any information economics.

In years ahead, the philosophical implications of these ideas will by themselves be inspiration for an encyclopedia of knowledge, as well as new social philosophies, political alignments, and more. As time passes, more new codes will undoubtedly be found or invented for microelectronic and biological uses.

Change will proceed rapidly in a new information-based economy. It will also be an information-based social system.

How to Look at Change

These are the ideas driving our era—ideas about information itself and how it drives people in ways never before imagined. In short, it is an era in which:

1. Value is assessed in terms of information.
2. Power is seen increasingly as the force of information and an agent of change and movement.
3. Both nature and society are being interpreted in terms of these values and forces.

In the coming decades, economies and nations will rise, prosper, and decline based primarily on their ability to use new information technologies. The implications of these changes are almost beyond imagining. It is not a mere matter of political change. We have already established in the presidency of Ronald Reagan—"The Great Communicator"—the ultimate value of communication to leadership. And this will be true regardless of political philosophy. We can already see a society building that is partly literate in information, but largely illiterate. We are beginning to see that value in the economy can be based on information.

If people choose, they can ignore information—or sit out the entire revolution, for that matter. This is practiced all the time in totalitarian countries—in the Soviet Union, for example, glasnost notwithstanding, whenever there is a disaster or embarrassing situation. (Remember the information blackout of the 1986 Chernobyl nuclear meltdown? Or the white South African government, desiring to keep the world, including its own citizens, ill-informed about the state of unrest?) Maintaining such societies demands that the coding system have a high degree of probability and very little creativity. It is likely that the "waiters" of information in such countries will tell you that, "The soup is quite good today," no matter how tasteless it may actually be.

Appendix
The National Media Index

The National Media Index (NMI) measures the major national media's coverage of specific issues on a biweekly basis. It tracks a set list of several hundred items, adding new ones as they appear. It can be useful to Trend Watchers in several ways. You can, for example, compare it with your own more finely tuned Trend-Watching data to view a trend on two levels: the broad national stage and your more specific interests. You can rely on its regular analysis to give you the larger picture, while you concentrate on the smaller worlds of importance to you. It can't be stated too often that effective Trend Watching requires you think both big and small and learn how to put the two views together.

At the end of this appendix you'll find the Issues List of the National Media Index—the detailed breakdown of subjects we track every week. This list can serve as a guide for developing your own set of issues. Also included are some sample graphs showing NMI data plotted two different ways. These data should be helpful in giving some insight into how national media trends have been moving. Don't be distressed if your own data are at variance with these broad-scale findings; both sets of data may be correct in their own way. And the combination of the two will give you an extra dimension of vision.

We have used NMI data at various stages in this book to describe national trends—those that affect the entire country. In general, the NMI is strongest in areas where the power of the major media is preeminent—in particular, foreign affairs, domestic politics, and government regulation.

Using the NMI Issues List

The NMI Issues List provides a framework of general news issues. You can use it, with additions, for your tracking of macro issues. If you examine the issues list, you will note that it is first broken into broad general categories: Government and Politics, Social Issues, Crime and Criminal Justice, Science and Resources, General Economics, and International Issues, among others. Each of these broad categories is broken down into subgroups, which are further divided into issue segments. By using a wide range of subsets, a vast amount of data has been regularly coded into the NMI data base. Let's examine the breakdown for the Health category:

5. Health
    A. Costs
        a. Insurance/benefits
    B. Medicare
    C. Drugs
    D. Disease control
        a. Smoking
        b. Cancer
        c. Herpes
        d. AIDS research
        e. AIDS fears
    E. Advances
        a. Transplants
        b. Biogenetics research
    F. Quality of care

        a. Military
    G. Fitness
        a. Diet

    While health is one of the fastest-growing areas of national
news, constantly changing in focus, this basic breakdown has
held up very well for Trend-Watching purposes over the years.
Even the addition of AIDS coverage is rare. Epidemics, after
all, don't come and go like fads; they tend to stick around for
a few decades. Note also that everything relating to health is
not necessarily found under this category. Pollution-borne diseases, for example, are cataloged under the Environment category:

1. Environment
        . . .

    D. Contamination
        a. Dioxin
        b. Agent orange
        c. Asbestos
        d. Pesticides, other
        e. Victim's compensation

Making good cross references is also a key factor in creating
an effective issues list. For more on this, see Chapter Five.
    To review, the National Media Index provides measure-
ments of major media. These reveal essentially four things:

1. They show which news is reaching the public. This
   measurement of total news flows indicates what Americans (and many Canadians) are hearing and reading
   about specific issues.
2. They show how the public is likely to respond. Because
   people act on what they know, the National Media Index
   provides insight into what the public is learning.
3. They show the impact on the media of issues and events.
   Measuring variations in coverage against a line of events,

we can gauge how important the media think an issue is. This is readily apparent when you compare the amount of coverage given succeeding events—plotting coverage of the president against his approval rating, for example, or the rise of public concern over an issue and subsequent congressional action on that subject.

4. They show what editors regard as news. While this may appear to be almost the same set of data already described, the results represent a unique aspect because editors influence each other.

The eleven media used in the National Media Index data base are the principal makers of the national consensus on news—the newspapers and news programs that are traditionally referred to as being "of record." They include:

1. The evening news shows of three television networks: ABC, CBS, and NBC
2. The three major national newsmagazines: *Newsweek, Time,* and *U.S. News & World Report*
3. The five leading newspapers with widespread networks of correspondents throughout the world, with major syndication services, and which, in turn, influence large sectors of news coverage: *Chicago Tribune, Los Angeles Times, New York Times, Wall Street Journal,* and *Washington Post*

Keep in mind that the National Media Index objectifies data by using numbers as a metaphor—in this case, for space and time. It is, at best, an inexact science. Because issue selection is itself a subjective matter, no index of this kind is ever more than an attempt to organize data more effectively to gain a better perspective.

Some Patterns

Over the years, certain patterns appear. For example:

• Any issue receiving more than 10 percent of all national coverage in any two-week period is seen as having reached the mass public. The number of such major stories is relatively small but growing each year.

- Regular, standby issues like the environment or social equity (often referred to as "fairness") have consistent ranges. The environment, for example, regularly receives about 2 percent of all media coverage.
- Major groups of issues tell a lot about how issues are competing with one another. The sharp drop in political coverage after the 1984 election and its revival in late 1986, for example, paints a vivid picture of change in the period.

The National Media Index is, if nothing else, a convenience for Trend Watchers. It serves as a benchmark, a calibrated measure against which other Trend-Watching activities can be compared and contrasted.

Tracking Major Issues

Figure A-1 is a graph showing the top twenty issues for two-week periods in January 1986 and 1987, as reported in *Issues Management Letter*. In particular, note the huge volume of coverage of the Iran-contra affair, which maintained just over 18 percent of all national media coverage for one entire quarter (November 1986–January 1987), an unprecedented level of coverage. The only thing comparable is the item immediately below it—criticism of the Reagan administration. This topic is a subset of the Iran-contra data, and, by itself, represented 14 percent of all news coverage during that quarter. This figure explains in part why approval ratings of an otherwise popular president dropped so precipitously—and remained down for so long.

Also note in Figure A-1 the relatively higher importance of corporate news (labeled "corporate governance" in the figure) in 1987 compared to the previous year. This marks a surprisingly large jump during the year in news about corporations, much of which was negative. Indeed, in the spring of

Figure A-1 Top twenty issues for two-week period, January 1986 and 1987.

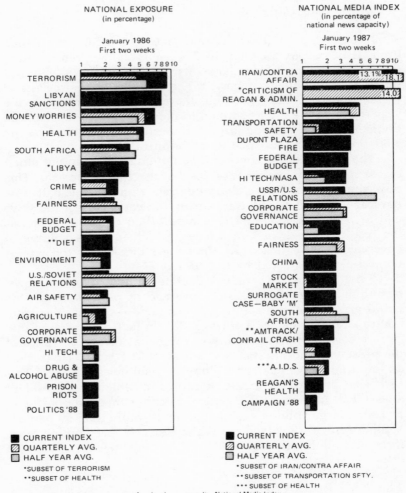

Note: Calculations based on percentage of national news capacity, National Media Index.

1987, such corporate negativism became the subject of voluminous column-inches and airtime.

Broad Issue Categories

Another way to look at trend data graphically is to map broad issue categories. Figure A-2 is one such map, representing the main headings of our issues list for the year 1986. Several things are immediately apparent. The bulge in "Resource" news (which includes high-tech and, therefore, space) early in the year reflected the attention paid to the loss of the space shuttle *Challenger*. This was the largest domestic story tracked by the NMI up to that time since its creation in 1982.

The second thing to note is the not-quite-so-steep but much bigger mountain labeled "Politics," at the end of the year. This peak shows two things: a sharp contrast with the unusually low coverage of politics received during the early part of the year, and a sharp rise *after* the November 1986 election. This was the result of the Iran-contra affair, which in gross volume of coverage easily eclipsed the *Challenger* disaster as the largest domestic story tracked by the NMI.

Finally, note the gradual decline of international news, beginning in October, as the coverage of politics rose. One could argue that some international news—that is, the Iran-contra affair—became "Politics." But, in fact, the focus of that story clearly shifted internally to the behavior and fortunes of the president and his staff and advisors. The White House lost an important advantage when international news declined. This had been an area of media attention in which the president always had had unusual leverage. Because international news had such large volume—taking, at times, more than 50 percent of all coverage—it served the White House by preempting more intractable domestic issues.

The NMI Issues List

These 300+ issues and subissues comprise the data base of the National Media Index. The list is constantly revised and updated

Figure A-2 Map of Broad Issues, January 12, 1986–January 11, 1987.

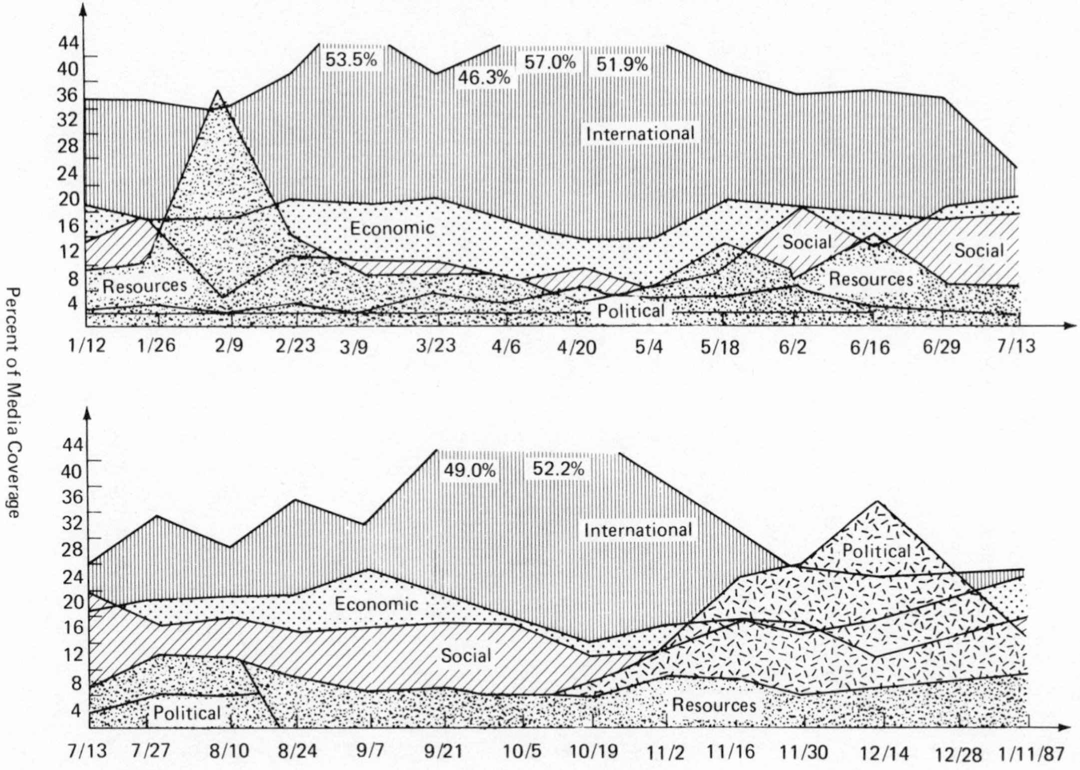

Percent of Media Coverage

to reflect the rise and fall of issues in the national media. You may find the list useful as a guide in compiling your own issues list. Keep in mind that compiling such a list involves as much art as science. There are a variety of ways to catalog every issue. The key to successful Trend Watching is to catalog consistently the same type story in the same way. This will provide the strongest, most reliable data base from which to track trends.

Domestic Issues

Government, Politics

1. Reagan, Criticism of
   A. Domestic policy
      a. Fairness
      b. Economic policy
   B. Foreign policy
      a. Arms policy
      b. Central America
      c. Mideast/Iran
      d. African policy
   C. Staff/White House
   D. Personal health
2. Administration, Criticism of
   A. Environmental policy
   B. Personnel
   C. Media relations, leaks
   D. Foreign policy
      a. Arms policy
      b. Central America
      c. Mideast/Iran
      d. African policy
3. Congress, Criticism of
4. Lobbying
   A. PACs

5. Political Parties
   A. GOP
   B. Democratic party
   C. Independent
6. Congressional Agenda
7. State/Local Politics
   A. Campaigns
   B. Corruption
   C. Gambling
      a. Lotteries

Social Issues

1. Fairness
   A. Civil rights
   B. Minorities
      a. Blacks
      b. Hispanics
      c. Jews
      d. Asians
   C. Women
      a. Politics
      b. Economics
   D. Federal programs
      a. Cuts
      b. Social Security
      c. Welfare/ subsidies

E. Poverty/homeless
  a. Churches
  b. Housing/
     shelters
F. Aging
G. Integration
  a. Affirmative
     action
  b. Busing
H. Racism
2. Education
  A. Standards/quality
    a. Math/science
    b. Bilingual
       education
  B. Funding/spending
  C. Teachers
    a. Merit pay
  D. Business involvement
  E. Higher education
    a. Costs
    b. Business
       inventory
    c. Student loans
    d. Athletes
  F. Discipline
3. Family
  A. Violence
    a. Child abuse
    b. Teen suicide
  B. Child care
    a. Daycare
    b. Missing kids
4. Drug/Alcohol Abuse
  A. Drunk driving
    a. Drinking age
  B. Athletes
  C. On the job

5. "Social" Issues
  A. Teen pregnancy
    a. Sex education
  B. Abortion
    a. Church
  C. Bioethics
    a. Church
  D. Morality/pornography
6. Privacy
7. Volunteerism
8. Military Draft
9. Immigration
  A. Illegal aliens
    a. Reform bill
    b. Sanctuary
       movement
  B. Assimilation
10. Religion in United States
  A. Church/state
    a. School prayer
  B. Catholic Church
  C. National Council of
     Churches
  D. Evangelism

Crime/Criminal Justice

1. Crime
  A. Youth
  B. Drug trafficking
    a. International
  C. White collar
    a. Insider trading
  D. Hi-tech
  E. Organized crime
    a. Money
       laundering

2. Criminal Justice
   A. Prisons
      a. Overcrowding
   B. Sentencing
      a. Capital
         punishment
      b. Parole
   C. Insanity defense
   D. Victims' rights
   E. Evidence
   F. Juvenile justice
3. Courts
   A. Juries
   B. Judges
   C. Supreme Court
   D. Lawyers
   E. Litigation
      a. malpractice
4. Gun Control

General Domestic

1. Media
   A. Criticism of
   B. Media takeovers
2. Census Reports
3. Natural Disasters
   A. Weather
      a. Flooding
      b. Fires
      c. Drought

Economic Issues

Science/Resources

1. Environment

A. Clean air
   a. Acid rain
   b. Lead
   c. Ozone
   d. Radon
B. Water
   a. Supply, other
   b. Supply, ground
   c. Quality, other
   d. Quality, ground
C. Waste/Superfund
D. Contamination
   a. Dioxin
   b. Agent orange
   c. Asbestos
   d. Pesticides, other
   e. Victim's
      compensation
E. Land use
F. Wildlife
2. Energy
   A. Oil
      a. Prices
      b. Supplies
   B. Gas
      a. Prices
      b. Supplies
   C. Utilities (nonrate)
   D. Other energy sources
      a. Synfuels
   E. Conservation
3. Nuclear Power
   A. Safety
   B. Costs
   C. Waste disposal
      a. Transport

4. Hi-tech/Research
   A. Information
      a. Computers
      b. Communications
   B. Space
      a. Shuttle
      b. Commercial
         development
   C. Competition
      a. International
      b. State and local
   D. Research
      a. Biotech
      b. Automation
      c. R&D
5. Health
   A. Costs
      a. Insurance/
         benefits
   B. Medicare
   C. Drugs
   D. Disease control
      a. Smoking
      b. Cancer
      c. Herpes
      d. AIDS research
      e. AIDS fears
   E. Advances
      a. Transplants
      b. Biogenetics
         research
   F. Quality of care
      a. Military
   G. Fitness
      a. Diet

General Economics

1. Negative Economic News
   A. Unemployment
      a. Jobs programs
   B. Bankruptcies
      a. Financial
         institutions
2. Positive Economic News
3. Budgets
   A. Federal
      a. Deficit
      b. Cuts
      c. Item veto
   B. Defense spending
      a. Pensions
   C. State budgets
4. Taxes
   A. Federal
      a. Corporate
   B. State
   C. Morality/evasion
   D. Federal reform
      a. Corporate
      b. Negative
         coverage
5. Labor
   A. Unions
   B. Strikes
   C. Wages/concessions
   D. Management
      relations
   E. Pensions/benefits
   F. Federal workers
   G. Worker safety
      a. Contamination
   H. Workers' rights

6. Trade
   A. Japan
      a. Auto
      b. Hi-tech
   B. East/west
   C. Protectionism
      a. Steel
   D. Agriculture
   E. Asia, other
   F. Dollar
   G. Deficit
   H. Canada
7. Economic Policy
   A. Industrial policy
   B. Supply side
8. Antitrust
   A. Mergers
   B. Takeovers
      a. Oil
   C. AT&T
9. Regulation
   A. FDA
   B. Health institutions
   C. Financial institutions
   D. Business
   E. Communications
   F. Transportation
      a. Railroads
      b. Airlines
   G. Energy/gas
10. Consumer Protection
    A. Auto
       a. Service
       b. Safety
    B. Air travel
       a. Service
       b. Safety

   C. Child safety
   D. Food safety
      a. Aspartame
      b. Salmonella
      c. Pesticides
   E. Drugs
      a. Bendectin
   F. Utility rates
      a. Phone rates
   G. Rail safety/service
11. Money
    A. FED
    B. Interest rates
    C. Inflation
       a. disinflation
    D. Stock market
    E. Banking institutions
    F. Gold
    G. Foreign investment
12. Corporate Governance
    A. Negative coverage
       a. Corruption
    B. Management
    C. Marketing
    D. Personnel
    E. Ethics
13. Privatization
14. Infrastructure
    A. Area development
    B. Transit
15. Agriculture
    A. Government policy/
       subsidies
    B. Economic news
16. Industrial Accidents
    A. Bhopal

B. Transport
C. Nuclear accidents
17. Issues Management
18. Real Estate
19. Advertising
20. Products in News

International Issues

1. Middle East
   A. Lebanon
      a. Government/
         army
      b. U.S. involvement
      c. Fighting
      d. Peace
         negotiations
   B. Palestinians
      a. PLO
      b. West Bank
   C. Israel
      a. Internal
      b. U.S. relations
   D. Syria
   E. Soviet involvement
2. Persian Gulf
   A. Iran/Iraq
   B. Iran
      a. U.S. involvement
3. Central America
      a. U.S. involvement
   A. El Salvador
      a. U.S. involvement
   B. Nicaragua
      a. U.S. involvement
   C. Guatemala
   D. Mexico

E. Honduras
   a. U.S. involvement
4. Caribbean
   A. Cuba
   B. Grenada
   C. Haiti
5. South America
   A. Argentina
   B. Brazil
   C. Chile
6. European Allies
   A. NATO
      a. United Kingdom
      b. France
      c. West Germany
      d. Italy
      e. Greece
      f. Spain
   B. Economic
   C. Espionage
7. Disarmament
   A. Freeze movement
   B. NATO
   C. Arms control talks
      a. ABM
   D. Churches
   E. Nonproliferation
   F. Chemical bans
8. USSR
   A. Leaders
   B. Economy
   C. Hi-tech
      a. Space program
      b. Chernobyl
   D. U.S./Soviet relations
      a. Arms race
      b. Espionage

9. U.S. Defense Policy
   A. Reforms
      a. Personnel
   B. Strategy
      a. "Star Wars," SDI
   C. Weapons
      a. Procurement
      b. Contractors/
         disputes
   D. Security
10. Eastern Bloc
   A. Poland
   B. Afghanistan
11. China
   A. Taiwan
   B. Sino/Soviet relations
   C. Hong Kong
12. Japan
   A. Economy
13. Southeast Asia
   A. Vietnam/Cambodia
      conflict
14. Korea
   A. North
   B. South
15. Philippines
16. India
17. World Economy
   A. Development/LDC's
   B. Recession
      a. Debt/IMF
      b. Population
      c. Hunger
   C. Recovery
   D. Labor
   E. Exchange
   F. Trade
18. United Nations
   A. U.S. role

19. Human Rights
   A. Soviet bloc
   B. Holocaust
   C. Latin America
20. World Religion
   A. Vatican
      a. Pope John Paul
      b. Political
         involvement
      c. Synod/Vatican II
21. Terrorism
   A. Domestic
      a. Abortion clinic
         bombings
      b. Racially
         prompted
   B. International
      a. Libya
      b. Israel
      c. Lebanon
      e. Europe
      f. Pope assasina-
         tion plot
      g. Abu Nidal
22. Canada
23. Ireland
24. Africa
   A. South Africa
      a. U.S. policy
      b. Disinvestment
   B. Libya
   C. Angola
25. Anzus
   A. Australia
   B. New Zealand
26. Espionage
27. Pakistan
29. World Health
   A. AIDS

The Conference on Issues and Media

The Conference on Issues and Media, Inc. was formed in 1982 to study and report on media coverage and its impact on public behavior. Since that time it has developed and maintained a variety of measurements of news flow. One of these, the National Media Index—the first computerized measurement of news from major national news media, including both television and print—is the source of data used in this book.

Data from the National Media Index are published biweekly in two newsletters, *Issues Management Letter* and *Corporate Exposure*. To obtain a free sample copy of either publication, write to: Conference on Issues and Media, Dept. B, Box 7498, Alexandria, VA 22307.

Index

CBS, 47, 53, 56, 58, 59–60, 61,
    98, 166, 189
  shift in coverage of liberal
    issues by, 59–60
CBS/New York Times poll, 38
chemical industry, 2, 10–13
Chemical Manufacturers
    Association, Trend Watching
    activities of, 12–13
Chernobyl nuclear accident, 43,
    44, 67, 143, 151, 158, 185
Chicago, 107
Chicago Tribune, 54, 67, 98, 107,
    124, 189
Chicago Tribune Company, 54
Christian Science Monitor, 53
Chrysler Corporation, 135
classified ads, 116
Coca-Cola, 1–2, 3, 4
comics, 116
Commentary, 110
communication, theories of,
    171–185
  see also information age
computers, in Trend Watching,
    109, 120
Congress, 12, 15, 154–155
  effect of media on, 75
constructs, in Trend Watching,
    137–139
consumer safety and protection,
    media coverage of, 149–151
Corporate Exposure (newsletter),
    ix
corporate personnel manager,
    issues list for, 90–92
corporations, media coverage of,
    138–139, 163–164, 169–170
countertrends, 137–139
counting and calculating,
    115–128

frequency of, 119
techniques, 118–120
who should do, 117
Crain's Chicago Business, 107
criticism of Reagan
    administration, coverage of,
    35
Cronkite, Walter, 56

demand for news, 56–59
Demography, 70
Denver Post, 108
Des Moines Register, 107
determining issues for Trend
    Watching, 77–94
Direct Selling Foundation, 48
discontinuities, spotting, 142–143
dominance of U.S. news
    organizations, 61–62
Dow Chemical, 2
drug abuse, media coverage of,
    133
Du Pont, 2–3, 6, 12, 135

economics, media coverage of,
    23–24, 50, 147–149, 154–155
  positive vs. negative, 169
Economist, 110, 111–112
economists as Trend Watchers,
    21–22
election campaign, issues list
    for, 87–90
elections, 17
  presidential, 134
  role of Trend Watching in,
    17–20
electronic media
  difficulties in using, for Trend
    Watching, 101
  role in Trend Watching,
    54–55, 99–101